# HEAD ON!

# HEAD ON!

## Collisions of Egos, Ethics, and Politics in B.C.'s Transportation History

R.G. Harvey

Library and Archives Canada Cataloguing in Publication

Harvey, R.G. (Robert Gourlay), 1922-
      Head on!: collisions of egos, ethics, and politics in B.C.'s transportation history/R.G. Harvey.

Includes bibliographical references and index.
ISBN 1-894384-75-X


      1. Transportation—Government policy—British Columbia—History.
2. Transportation—British Columbia—History. 3. British Columbia—Politics and government. I. Title.

HE215.Z7B715 2004          388'.09711          C2004-905046-X

Cover photo: The Heritage House Collection.
Cover design: Nancy St.Gelais.
Book design and layout: Darlene Nickull.
Editors: Karla Decker and Paula Johanson.

Heritage House acknowledges the financial support for its publishing program from the Government of Canada through the Book Publishing Industry Development Program (BPIDP), Canada Council for the Arts, and the Province of British Columbia through the British Columbia Arts Council.

Heritage House Publishing Ltd.
#108-17665 66A Ave.
Surrey, BC, Canada
V3S 2A7
greatbooks@heritagehouse.ca
www.heritagehouse.ca

Printed in Canada

BRITISH
COLUMBIA
ARTS COUNCIL
We acknowledge the support of the Province of British Columbia
through the British Columbia Arts Council

The Canada Council | Le Conseil des Arts
for the Arts | du Canada

This book is dedicated to my family—for them "long-suffering" is a word not sufficiently descriptive.

# Acknowledgements

My thanks go out to all at Heritage House, particularly Karla Decker, and to Paula Johanson.

*"Historical memory is the only dependable guide for any rational navigation into the unknown waters of an uncertain future."*

—Anthony J. Hall

# Contents

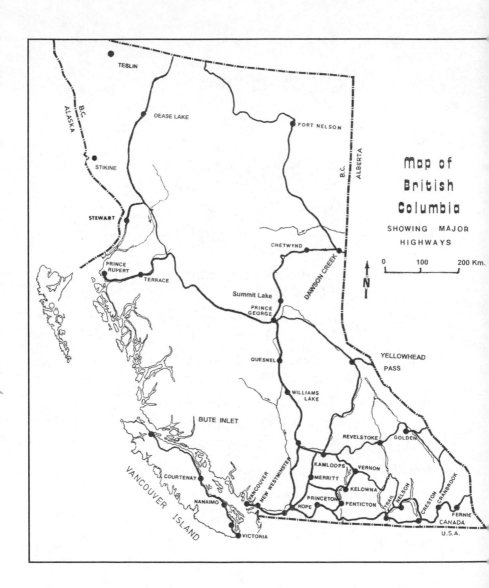

Map of British Columbia

SHOWING MAJOR HIGHWAYS

# Preface

Throughout its history, British Columbia's successive premiers have gotten themselves into trouble in their handling of transportation issues, and in the ways they have responded to their mandates. Almost all of them exploited their time in office to advance their own political preferences, and while they often committed similar errors, they managed to find their own unique ways of getting into poor political health due to their decisions on railways, roads, or ferries—ailments that were almost always terminal. The recurring pattern in B.C. has been a series of head-on collisions between political ambitions, egos, and ethics when it came to providing means of movement throughout the province from its very first days.

While this book is in some ways a sequel to my first look at B.C.'s transportation history in *The Coast Connection*, my goal here is to look at the premiers and their ministers of public works or highways from the viewpoint of their errors rather than their achievements in the field. While there is no shortage of errors to focus on, deciding which premiers performed well and which didn't in fulfilling their mandates and building the province's infrastructure is a complicated matter.

B.C.'s longest-serving premier, W.A.C. Bennett, for example, certainly seemed to have been on the right course in solving Vancouver Island's transportation challenges by proposing a shorter ferry route. But then, who conceived and started building the Dease Lake rail line, three-laned the Pat Bay Highway, and brought in a promoter who promised to build a monorail up the Rocky Mountain Trench?

Still, Bennett was undoubtedly the most successful of all B.C.'s premiers. Why? Because he was one of the very few (others include Oliver, Pattullo, Hart, and Johnson) who shied away from the politics of exploitation, something that has dominated the performance of most of the province's leaders. Political exploitation, as the term is used here, means using one's time in office to seek and support fully political objectives, as opposed to seeking the general good of the province's people. Some of this is acceptable and necessary, of course, but an excess of it is not, and leads to extreme polarization. British Columbians suffer more than other Canadians this way, because we tend to elect heads of government who are more controversial than complaisant.

To quote Edwin R. Black, professor of political science at Queens University, in his article "The Politics of Exploitation," "The province's politics are notable for their lack of traditionalism and for their instability. This arises from the notorious unpredictability of British Columbia's premiers, the tumultuousness of the partisan fray, and the voter's fickleness about party allegiance."[1]

W.A.C. Bennett was certainly unpredictable at times, but towards one goal he was not: he excelled in boosting the economy of the province. To accomplish this, he would lean either to the left or the right, whatever was most expedient—hence his motto, "progress, not politics." As well as the generation of electric power, his achievement for the greater good was the construction of highways and the ferries. Professor Black writes about how this affected small businesses (Bennett's "people"): "Highways are of enormous economic benefit to small-scale operators, are of great utility in relieving feelings of desperation and frustration in isolated people, and are simply good politics."

In retrospect, we can now appreciate that the benefits of W.A.C. Bennett's leadership and policies far outweighed the costs in many respects.[2] And since transportation was his prime concern, it is appropriate that this should be the focus for our examination of B.C.'s premiers and their errors and exploitations.

## Chapter One

# The Parade of Premiers:
# 1871 to 1903

*"The government of an exclusive company of merchants is, perhaps, the worst of all governments."*
—Adam Smith, Wealth of Nations, 1776

*"A civil service queerly recruited, and commanded by a group of piddling premiers!"*
—Gilbert Martin Sproat, 1909

The matter of transportation was much on the minds of the citizens of British Columbia when they joined Confederation—and in those days transportation meant railways. Neither John Foster McCreight nor Amor De Cosmos distinguished themselves in that respect, but they were not unscathed by the furore over the route choice for the promised transcontinental railway, either through the Coast Mountains by the Fraser River Canyon, or by way of Bute Inlet. All provincial politicians at that time were affected by the politics of the route choice.

McCreight, an English lawyer who was in office from November 1871 to December 1872, was described as "bad tempered and queer" and "utterly ignorant of politics" by Governor Douglas' erstwhile attorney general, Henry Crease.[1] He was Lieutenant-Governor Joseph William Trutch's choice for the first premier of the province, and these personality traits probably led to his early removal. His 13 months as premier were quite undistinguished, and they ended, as became virtually a tradition for ex-premiers who were lawyers, with a senior appointment to the bench.

As the Supreme Court justice responsible for the Cariboo and Barkerville, McCreight travelled the Cariboo Road constantly. On one trip he experienced the first indication of how adversely the new CPR main line would affect the Fraser Canyon roadway when railway surveyors disturbed rocks, which then fell onto the road. The stagecoach in which the judge was travelling very nearly went into the river. McCreight vociferously blamed the department of lands and works for the incident.

After McCreight came the legendary Amor De Cosmos, a journalist, a native of Nova Scotia, and a reformer to the core who championed British Columbia to the utmost. Sadly, he proved to be an unstable man at times, one in whom a fertile imagination led to a name change—his name at birth was William Alexander Smith. His short stay in office (about 14 months) was so consumed by conflict over the terms of reference for Confederation, and the route for the national railway, the bait for joining Canada, that few of his errors or exploitations can be singled out.

For some of the time he was both the premier of the province and member of Parliament for Victoria. His constant arguing with Edgar Dewdney, the MP for Yale, was on both fronts, about whether or not British Columbia should come into Canada as well as about the route for the westernmost end of the Canadian Pacific Railway: Bute Inlet versus the Fraser Canyon, the first leading to Victoria, the second to Vancouver. Those in favour of Victoria rather than Vancouver as the terminus seemed to be quite blind to the fact that Burrard Inlet would make a much better harbour than would Esquimalt. Dewdney was tempted to take both a seat in the national government and also a seat in Victoria and the post of attorney general. However, De Cosmos attacked him when it seemed he would do this, on the basis that he was disenfranchising one set of voters against the other—apparently he did not feel that this applied to himself![2]

Amor De Cosmos, the second premier (December 1872 to February 1874) was the first one from the fourth estate. He brought little of his first name to the position, as he was involved in turmoil almost constantly while in office. In his later, more placid years, his proposals for transportation were often visionary but, unfortunately, unachievable.

De Cosmos started two daily newspapers, the *British Colonist*, which he sold, then the *Standard*, both published in Victoria. At about the time that the *Standard* shut down in 1890, he was promoting the Victoria, Saanich, and New Westminster Railway. This proposal was a rather eerie precursor to the Swartz Bay-to-Tsawwassen ferry route, because both would take to the water at Swartz Bay, and the railway was proposed to come to shore on the mainland at English Bluffs close to Tsawwassen. Sadly it never left the planning stage. It could have led to a night train to Victoria instead of a night boat.[3]

George Anthony Walkem, the member for Cariboo, succeeded De Cosmos in 1874. He stayed in the hazardous and mostly tempo-rary job until 1876, and then again from 1878 to 1882, with Andrew

George Anthony Walkem, the third and fifth premier (February 1874 to January 1876 and June 1878 to June 1882), was once described by Governor General Lord Dufferin as intellectually frail—a tactful but deadly condemnation. Walkem was a consummate fence-sitter, as was his fellow premier from the Cariboo, Charles Semlin—maybe the Cariboo's rail fences encouraged that. He was the only premier entering twice into office. He had been chief commissioner of lands and works under McCreight.

Charles Elliot serving in between as a calm interlude. Walkem was another toe-to-toe combatant with Dewdney, although Dewdney despised Walkem for his stubborn stupidity, a feeling he certainly did not have for De Cosmos.[4]

Railways had become political footballs. To appease the good people of Vancouver Island, the great minds in Ottawa brazenly put forward a proposal for an Island railway from Esquimalt to Nanaimo, but Walkem would not have it. He wanted the main line to come down Bute Inlet and to terminate on Vancouver Island and nowhere else. In his first term of office, while furiously differing with the national government but at the same time not hesitating to borrow money from it, he started on a huge program of public works, focussing mostly on roads. This effort came close to bankrupting the young province, and it brought along Walkem's removal. Dismissal of premiers was almost a routine thing by the lieutenant-governors in those early years.

During Elliot's tenure, it was decided that the transcontinental railway would go by the Fraser Canyon. On Walkem's return to office in 1878, his fury at the decision led him to an act against the railway builders that was suicidal for a politician. He imposed a thoroughly unwise road toll of $10 per ton on all freight using the Cariboo Road through the Fraser Canyon. This seriously impoverished his constituents in the Cariboo, who were dependent upon that road and its wagon trains for supplies. It also infuriated the aristocratic contractor for the railway, Andrew Onderdonk, who was a good man for the province's first minister to be friendly with at that time. Predictably, Walkem departed his high office for the second time soon after that, his departure being eased along by the standard atonement for a lawyer, an appointment to the Supreme Court.

One interesting result of Walkem's stubbornness was a colourful incident in the history of B.C.—that of the sternwheeler SS *Skuzzy* taking on the Fraser River. This vessel, launched by Andrew Onderdonk in May 1882, was equipped with a powerful engine and multiple waterproof bulkheads. It was built to challenge the current and the other hazards of Black Canyon and Hells Gate, in order to haul freight through the Fraser Canyon without paying the road toll. This was successfully achieved. The inaugural trip was witnessed by Onderdonk and his guests from an excursion train on the track above. Walkem privatized the maintenance of the Cariboo Road in 1881, but this was not a success, and the responsibility for maintenance reverted to the civil service in 1887.[5]

The next man up was Robert Beaven (1882–1883), a real estate agent in private life and a man of solemn mien leading a weak coalition of supporters. He provided a government fully open to domination by the province's capitalists, particularly by Robert Dunsmuir, Vancouver Island's coal tycoon. Not content with the wealth he already had, Dunsmuir wanted to acquire more by means of well-compensated railway construction and grants of the land and mineral rights around it. He got all that he wanted.

The one great fault with the provincial government at that time was the almost complete lack of continuity in leadership. There were 6 premiers in 12 years, followed by 1 for 4 years, and then another 8 in 16 years. What was at fault was the system. The lieutenant-governor appointed the member of the legislature with the most supporters as the premier minister, and then that man appointed his friends to the various offices of attorney general, chief commissioner of lands and works, and so on.

Another problem was that without party organization, there was no discipline—all of them were free to leave their leader at any time and to plot against him thereafter. As soon as there were sufficient dissidents to bring about the repeated defeat of motions put to the House by the premier, the harassed lieutenant-governor had to

Robert Beaven, B.C.'s sixth premier (June 1882 to January 1883) was one of the first to have worked in real estate before his election (Bill Bennett was a later one). A lacklustre leader, he was nonetheless clairvoyant in predicting a highway link eastwards. His later career as mayor of Victoria came to a sudden end in 1896 when the Point Ellice Bridge collapsed, taking a train and numerous citizens to a watery grave.

find another majority leader, and thereby another governing group. It was not until 1903 that the party system was imported from the East, to the great relief of all concerned.

In 1882 Robert Beaven should have been well aware of the hazards of transportation issues for lawmakers, given that he had been chief commissioner of lands and works from 1872 to 1876. Beaven was interested in roads, particularly the construction of what became known as the Old Yale Road, from Ladner to Yale. This was a pet project of his, but an unfortunate one. His opponent was the Fraser River, which would have none of it, washing it out decisively in the floods of 1874 and 1876. While probably not the prime cause for his departure from the premier's job six years later after only 7½ months in office, certainly the failure to make this a permanent roadway did not add to his stature.

It is evident that even in these early years of the province's history, political enemies, the system, the national government, and the natural elements all conspired against British Columbia's premiers in matters of transportation. Beaven displayed remarkable insight when he predicted that at some time in the future there would be a road through the Cascade Mountains through the Coquihalla River valley. He did this in a speech to the legislature in 1882,[6] when he was both premier and chief commissioner of lands and works, a combination of duties often preferred then because of the patronage powers of the lesser position. Such a road did not become a reality for another hundred years, but it was a good idea, as the present Coquihalla Highway demonstrates. It is by far the most successful toll highway in B.C.'s history, taking in $42 million in tolls in the year 2000.

After Beaven came William Smithe. He became known as the man of peace, which was probably why he stayed in office for four years. With peace came compromise with those on Vancouver Island; while Walkem had fought strenuously with the national government over the transcontinental railway, and Elliot and Beaven had shilly-shallied, Smithe climbed right into bed with the Canadian Pacific Railway, which became a reality across the province to the Lower Mainland during his term in office.

This lover of railways inaugurated his transportation policy by closing down all road building other than on Vancouver Island,

William Smithe, the seventh premier (January 1883 to March 1887) was the first one to realize the advantages of giving away British Columbia's best land to achieve his political goals. Smithe gave many acres of it to a pair of transportation pioneers: the CPR and Gustavus Blin Wright. Neither generous gift gained him any credit.

an action he never would have survived were it not for the euphoria felt by all towards the iron horse. In 1884 the CPR's William Cornelius Van Horne, probably one of the most influential and dominating corporate chief executive officers there has ever been in Canada's history, made his celebrated expedition to British Columbia. Met by the fawning Premier Smithe, Van Horne promptly demanded a huge dedication of provincial land, free of charge, along the south shore of Burrard Inlet. If the province did not comply, he threatened to stop further construction and have the terminus remain at Port Moody, the tidewater point reached by the railway at that time.[7]

Because there were several burgeoning timber mills already on that shore and they all wanted access to the main line, Smithe immediately gave in. The CPR received over 6,000 acres of prime waterfront land, free of charge and free of taxation for many years to come. In addition, the accommodating premier arranged for a lease dedication of 4,000 additional acres to the CPR, from such rights held by these same timber companies. In return for this the premier obtained the enmity of the Port Moody merchants, whose location suffered an immediate setback. The suspicion of all in the province was that this new servant of the people, the CPR, would in many ways become their master—a prophecy not lacking in fulfilment. The irony of this was, of course, the fact that the CPR could never have ended at Port Moody in any case, since that area of Burrard Inlet had mud flats and shallow water, and the railway needed deep water for ocean-vessel access. Deep water was only available further west on the inlet; thus the great harbour city of Vancouver was founded.[8]

Smithe was not satisfied with the extent of his surrender to the new way of travel. He also conspired in at least one other way to help the railway builders along—and at the same time assuage his conscience for his lack of road building in the Interior. He granted a charter to a well-known (and legendary) road builder, Gustavus Blin Wright, to build a road from Sicamous to Revelstoke, just before construction was about to start on the railway between these points; both were on a routing through Eagle Pass. To pay for this, the cash-strapped premier employed a favourite device of B.C. politicians when short of funds: the dispossession of publicly owned land in order to avoid the closer examination that use of treasury funds would have involved. In return, G.B. Wright received a grant of 60,000 acres of prime land, beside the railway and around Revelstoke, to be sold in 160-acre parcels to the settlers who were sure to come with the railway.

Wright carried out his part and even contributed a ferry across the Columbia River at Revelstoke to serve his customers. The CPR was of course the major beneficiary, because it received, quite free of charge, an access road through mountainous territory to aid its construction. But the road did not remain usable for long—and some said it was barely a road. After the rail line was built, it fell into neglect and in a few years disappeared. Eventually it was recreated, when the monopoly of rail travel wore thin, and it is now part of the Trans-Canada Highway.

In this way, the CPR took over as the only avenue of transportation through the Monashee Mountains. The railway company wanted no competition from a road, and the provincial government of William Smithe complied in every way that it could. Reaction arose quite soon, however, when prospective settlers found out that instead of receiving this Crown land free of charge as most settlers did in those days, they had to pay good money for it to Gus Wright. Smithe had delayed any sitting of the legislature for many months to avoid having to explain his railway concessions, but was finally forced to call a sitting in the spring of 1887. His fear of facing the music for his actions was swiftly allayed by his premature death on March 29 of that year.[9]

While no one could say that B.C.'s provincial government was totally corrupt in its first 32 years of existence, weakness at the top led to dalliance with the perquisites of power, not only by those in the government but also by those close to them. When Premier Smithe gave away land to the CPR on a huge scale, others thought they should benefit similarly. One example of this in Smithe's time concerned Lieutenant-Governor Hugh Nelson (1887-1892). He held a major interest in a logging company that happily leased 17 square miles of choice coastal timber land for a fee of one cent per acre. This strategy of using Crown land as a means towards gaining political advantage carried on with the following premiers, although John Robson did show some responsibility when he abolished the custom of including water and mineral rights, a move greatly resented in the Kootenays.

Historian Margaret Ormsby did some excellent research. Robert E. Cail, one of her students, combed through the lands-branch records and found that in 1899, under Premier Charles Semlin, two Victoria merchants (who shall ever remain nameless) submitted a plan (virtually just a line on a map) for a railway to be built on Crown land between Yellowhead Pass and Nanaimo, B.C., and applied for a charter for this purpose. To get it, they needed the support of a private member of Parliament in Ottawa for a railway bill, which they got, then the endorsement of a senator for a supply statute, which they also acquired, and the deed was done. The charter included unused, and in many areas unusable, Crown land for a generous width either side of their line on the map, and the total area granted from Yellowhead to Nanaimo was 18 million acres. Thanks to Premier Robson, at least they did not get the water and mineral rights. The final disposition of this land is not clear.[10]

This rip-off of land and other benefits in the matter of railways continued, and always involved those at the top. Another historian, Marjorie C. Holmes, demonstrated this in her article for the *B.C. Historical Quarterly* in October 1944. She described one commission formed under the Public Inquiries Act from a resolution brought by Smith Curtis, MLA for Rossland, on March 19, 1902. The resolution was brought against James Dunsmuir (Robert's son and then-premier) and certain members of his cabinet in respect to a planned rail line from Bute Inlet to Yellowhead Pass involving the Esquimalt and Nanaimo Railway and the Comox and Cape Scott Railway—a line that existed on paper only.

The resolution asserted that James Dunsmuir and his colleagues in cabinet were planning to give the Canadian Northern Railway an excessive subsidy of money and lands to build a line from Bute Inlet to Yellowhead Pass. It said that this was done "with a view to the sale at a greater price than could otherwise be got of the E & N and Comox & Cape Scott railways and their rights …" It also stated that as a heavy shareholder in these companies, James Dunsmuir would reap the benefit. The evidence was said to be dramatic. The commission was adjourned before doing anything, and there the record ceases. Dunsmuir resigned on November 21, 1902; he may have done so in part due to this indiscretion, although nothing

Always in the dark shadow of Robert Dunsmuir, son James (B.C.'s 14th premier, from June 1900 to November 1902) did somewhat better for British Columbia, although he was a reluctant premier put in to fill a gap. Political manipulation of provincial lands for personal benefit by way of railways did not succeed as well for him as it had done for his father.

came of the railway.[11] Once again, it seems transportation may well have gotten a premier into trouble.

In our parade of premiers, William Smithe's successor, Alexander Edmund Batson Davie, was the first of two to have this last name. Davie was politically overwhelmed by Robert Dunsmuir's entry into politics. Dunsmuir, having decided to press the government from within instead of without, was elected for Nanaimo in 1887 and became the president of the council in Davie's cabinet. While this position was not as powerful as that of the premier, it was next to it, and this was a powerful man. Davie had no difficulty getting into trouble over railways with Dunsmuir alongside him. Five years prior to this, the "king of coal" in B.C. had been handsomely rewarded by the national government to do something about railways on Vancouver Island in order to offset the jealousy of the Islanders about the CPR on the mainland.[12]

By the Act of Agreement in 1883 between Ottawa and Victoria (more specifically, with Dunsmuir and his group), the Dominion offered 2 million acres of land and $750,000, plus mineral rights for coal—all in exchange for building a rail line through not exceptionally difficult terrain. The offer was taken up.

Our coal baron lived happily thereafter, but only for another three years, during which he built Craigdarroch Castle in Victoria, bought up companies right and left, and did virtually nothing good with his money. He represented the worst side of capitalism, mistreating his employees to the point of endangering their lives. The most disturbing example of this was his denial to employees of any protection against the dreaded firedamp in his mines because he deemed the needed safeguards too expensive. He did this while providing protective equipment for the supervisors. Neither the elder Dunsmuir nor the son who took over from him had any idea at all about fairness in labour relations. Robert Dunsmuir died in 1889.

By 1889, after both Dunsmuir and Davie had gone, John Robson had taken over. He immediately came face to face with another railway issue. This one involved neither the CPR main line (except indirectly) nor the E & N, but instead the pressing desire of certain Vancouver interests to gain a share of the wealth being taken out of the ground in the Kootenays at the end of the century, mostly by

John Robson, the ninth premier (August 1889 to June 1892), was a New Westminster newspaper owner who vented his wrath upon Governor Douglas without respite. He finally sold his *British Columbian*, moved to Victoria, and took up real estate, becoming an MLA and then B.C.'s ninth premier. Blood poisoning from an accident with a carriage door in London made him the only premier to be literally, not politically, done in by transportation. As with most premiers, a town was named after him, although a small one. The mountain was named after someone else.

Americans. The Vancouverites desperately wanted a rail line from the Kootenays to the coast to supplant the long roundabout route via Revelstoke and the Arrow Lakes. Added to this was the widespread dislike of American railway builders, many of whom were then active in the Kootenays. Robson was in a "no win" position here, and about all that he achieved before he left office was a ban on a spur line entering Nelson from the south. Foreign railway builders had to situate their terminal five miles out of town.

In 1892 Robson handed over power to Theo Davie, A.E.B.'s brother. Robson and Davie (premier from July 1892 to March 1895) were each in office for three years, which was about the standard span of time between elections then, unless the lieutenant-governor needed to call one sooner due to misbehaviour. Robson and Davie both struggled with transportation problems. Theodore Davie was a very successful criminal defence lawyer who had been attorney general under Robson, and he continued his defence work with the government as his client. In the Supreme Court he successfully defended against an action by the CPR to quash a huge land-tax payment levied against them by his brother Alexander when he had been premier. This was in excess of $60,000, a huge amount in those days. When Theo became premier, he took further action in defence against the CPR: this time toward their monopoly of railway transportation in British Columbia. He co-operated fully with the national government in granting access to the American Great Northern Railway to build a line within the province from near Osoyoos to the coast.[13]

It was left to the next man to swing the pendulum back in favour of Canadian railway interests, and that man, John Herbert Turner, a stalwart supporter of the B.C. capitalist establishment, really got into trouble doing just that. Not only did Turner have to deal with the Kootenay mining boom, his term of office also contained the greatest transportation and social upset of them all, the Klondike gold rush. He came into office in March 1895, and had only been there 18 months when the first blow fell late in 1896. In that year the Dominion government signed the Crow's Nest Agreement with the CPR, giving substan-

John Herbert Turner, the 11th premier (March 1895 to August 1898) decided at the last minute before an election that building railways in the far north would sway the vote in his favour. Unfortunately for him, the first long-distance telegraph line of the province brought the news that his contractors had built several miles of rail line in the Bear Creek valley out of Stewart before discovering that the pass they were aiming for was blocked by a glacier. This rather significant oversight turned out to be Turner's terminal error; he was trounced at the polls.

tial freight-rate concessions to the prairie farmers. This was done at the expense of both the Canadian and British Columbian taxpayer, and it was a body blow to the newly energized Lower Mainland industrial leaders hoping to export their products eastwards at a favourable freight cost. It took them no time at all to realize that these favourable rates would subsidize others.[14]

Led by their mayor, the business community in Vancouver reacted with absolute fury and at once sought counteraction. This took the form of a charter for a rail line from the coast to Rossland B.C to compete with the CPR main line. The charter was taken out in the names of interested parties from Victoria and Vancouver, including Mayor Templeton.[15] In those days, charters for rail lines were handed out like political handshakes, and 99 out of 100 were never built. But this one was different. It was for the Vancouver, Victoria and Eastern Railway and Navigation Company, a cumbersome name that was quickly shortened to VV & E. Premier Turner of course immediately became a part of this, because any politician who did not involve himself in railways soon left office. [16]

In his dealings with this charter, Turner was to encounter the two most productive rail line promoters that Canada ever had, William Mackenzie and Donald Mann, eventually Sir William and Sir Donald. Originally contractors for the CPR main line, Mackenzie and Mann had branched out across Canada after that construction ended, building spur lines on the Prairies for farmers who desperately wanted rail access. For this work, "M & M" were paid well.

They finally extended their activity to the building of a through rail line across the northern Prairies named the Canadian Northern Railway, the same company that had gotten James Dunsmuir into trouble in 1902. But when they had met with Turner five years earlier, it was not about a rail line by Bute Inlet, it was about this much-desired line from the Kootenays to the coast.

Turner was no man of vision in this. He was a desperate politician faced with many transportation problems and an election looming. He had to do something to assure the Vancouver businessmen that the Kootenays were a part of B.C. and not a part of the U.S.A., which they really seemed to be at that time. He had to convince them that access along the U.S. border was possible for a railway and that he was working on it. On top of that, he had to convince everyone in B.C. that their provincial government was doing its utmost to assure a feasible route to the Klondike gold by the same means. He had a huge challenge!

Mackenzie and Mann bought out Mayor Templeton and his partners late in 1896, acquiring the VV & E charter at a cost of $75,000. With this they got the premier's full attention—not for a long-term solution, but for a quick fix. Several tentative contracts for railway construction were drawn up: Two would run between Vancouver and Rossland, B.C., despite the fact that Mackenzie and Mann had told Turner some years earlier that any railway building from the coast to the Kootenays was far from easy. One contract would run from the northern coast of B.C. toward the Yukon border, and one from that border to the south. One of the contracts was from Penticton to Rossland; another from Penticton to Vancouver; the third from Stewart, B.C. northeasterly towards Teslin Lake; the fourth southwesterly from there. Teslin Lake and Teslin River led to the Yukon valley. In spite of the vast area to be covered, all of these contracts were with the same individuals! [17]

Reaction in the Kootenays to the contracts in that area was quick to come, primarily from a powerful American, the mining czar from Montana, Fritz Heinze. He had just built a line into Rossland from south of the border, and he had also built the smelter for Rossland ore at Trail Creek by the Columbia River. He immediately announced that he too would build a rail line from Rossland to Penticton. Both contenders willing to surmount the very difficult Monashee mountains and Okanagan highlands at once decamped to Ottawa seeking a subsidy, the standard precursor to building a railway in those days. Mackenzie and Mann had already received a promise of $4,000 a mile from the province, but they needed much more than that from the national government. Both were turned down flat.

Despite all of this, by the summer of 1898 work had commenced in both areas under the direction of Mackenzie and Mann. Their procedure was well established: First promote the line (and they always worked with premiers in the provinces, never anyone else), then make a quick start, even on a small scale, and usually long before the final surveying and design was complete. Despite their competence in railway construction and their know-how in design gained from experience on the CPR main line, this sometimes led to extreme embarrassment when they encountered the unknown.

It certainly did on the Klondike line, which they started out of Stewart in the south and from Teslin Lake in the north. Work at Stewart went well that summer, just before the provincial election of August of 1898. They completed 40 miles of grading up the Bear River valley before they looked ahead. To their dismay they realized that across Bear Pass, their only way through the Coast Mountains, lay the Bear Glacier. There was no way at all that a railway could pass around, over, or through that barrier. Luckily for them, they were saved by the election, wherein John Herbert Turner's government was soundly defeated and the project was closed down.

In the south their efforts were less accelerated, and all that they achieved was the surveying and preliminary construction from the government wharf at the bottom of Okanagan Lake through Penticton and onwards for a very few miles towards Midway.[18] After the election everything came to a halt; transportation had once more struck a fatal blow to a B.C. premier.

Turner left office after a bitter dispute with the lieutenant-governor. He was soon to become B.C.'s agent general in London, and he proved to be much better at that job than the one as premier. Mackenzie and Mann departed Stewart, and they changed their agendas quickly to become the proponents of another way through the coastal range, that of the Stikine River. For this they found a

better partner—the CPR (albeit the sternwheeling branch)—with which to approach Ottawa, but this too was a promotion of theirs that came to nought. The Stikine River-to-Teslin proposal to access the Klondike fell apart when the legislation to support Mackenzie and Mann's rail line from Telegraph Creek to Teslin Lake was shot down by the Canadian Senate. The proposal had involved the British Columbia Lake and River Service, which was to run sternwheelers from the coast up the Stikine River to Telegraph Creek. The railway and steamboat conglomerate lost heavily on this aborted venture.[19]

B.C.'s 12th premier, Charles Augustus Semlin (August 1898 to February 1900), was a cattle rancher from Cache Creek and a man who did not like trouble. Semlin tried to appease both left and right in a tumultuous House; he ended up being condemned by both, as well as by an enraged public. He did, however, make the first moves to stop outrageous land bonuses for railway developers.

After Turner left, the revolving door to the premier's office started spinning again. Charles Augustus Semlin was the next man in, and he only lasted for about 20 months. He was in

Joe Martin, the 13th premier (February 1900 to June 1900), was a forthright individual. He was the first of the early premiers who seemed to have concern for the common man and to say so. He never sat in his seat at the head of the House because James Dunsmuir and his clique had him dismissed before the legislature came into session. He had planned to reorganize public works totally, a move sorely needed at that time.

charge when the previously described giveaway of 18 million acres to the proponents of a railway from Yellowhead Pass to Nanaimo took place—a proposal that was mysteriously quashed. He was followed by another of the colourful "head hombres" of B.C. of those days, Joseph Martin, or "Fighting Joe," as he was called.

Martin never did sit in the legislature in the premier's chair; he was dismissed by the lieutenant-governor after only a few months in office and before the House met. Despite his short stay, he found time to draw up a plan to completely overhaul public works, a proposal put together with consummate skill. In addition to this, he was prepared to proceed with a government-owned railway from the coast to the Kootenays. In view of all these good intentions, it was too bad he left; unfortunately, it seemed he never met anyone that he did not antagonize!

It could be said with some truth that he might have been the first representative of the common man in the premier's office, a point he emphasized when he announced that he was not going to be silenced by these "hobos in evening dress!" His problem, not a new one to premiers in those days, was a competitor for the leading role in the production of turmoil at the top in British Columbia: the lieutenant-governor—specifically, Lieutenant-Governor Thomas Robert McInnes, who was in office from 1897 to 1900.

Before getting into what was called "the McInnes incident," it is useful to discuss the function of the lieutenant-governor, a position

B.C.'s lieutenant-governor from 1897 to 1900, Thomas Robert McInnes was a medical doctor who later had become an MP. McInnes was one of the Port Moody investors who lost out when the CPR moved its final and most prestigious rail terminal to the outer end of Burrard Inlet. Switching parties to support Prime Minister Laurier's Liberals, he thereby fell into his high office in British Columbia, but fell out of it when he continued to play politics.

much more consequential to the business of governing than it appears to be when things go as they should. It is when things go wrong that the lieutenant-governor uses his powers; first when a premier seriously misbehaves, or second, when a premier ends up without a clear majority after an election. In the first case, he has the power to dismiss the premier and call an immediate election, along with the power to appoint an acting premier in the interim, if necessary.

In the second case, he has the power to call another election. But in the years we are now considering, when there was no political-party organization, that could prove to be most difficult. The lieutenant-governor might dismiss the premier in charge and appoint the leader of the largest group, believing they may have usurped the majority rule of those in power in the first place, even if that group had no clear majority. He would do this hoping that a more dominant leadership would win more support within a reasonable time. Obviously this was a very unsatisfactory outcome and one that any lieutenant-governor would dread.

McInnes came into office during John Turner's premiership, and when the votes were counted in the 1898 election, he and Turner crossed swords. Of the 38 seats in the House, Turner's supporters had won only 17. However, probably because of the pandemonium underway in northern B.C., with everyone rushing off to the Klondike, the election of 2 seats up there had not taken place when the returns for the rest of the province came in. In addition, 29 protests of irregularity were received for the seats that were elected. The voters of mainland B.C. had just had their members increased to 24, but their satisfaction about that quickly disappeared when they sensed double-dealing, and they demanded that Turner's government be thrown out. His government was seen by those in Vancouver to represent industrialists and capitalists centred in Victoria and to have been extravagantly generous to their friends with land grants and other benefits, to the extent of an $8 million deficit.[20]

Turner appears to have been one of B.C.'s more innovative premiers. Certainly many B.C. premiers have faked up short-term transportation projects in the hope of gaining re-election through them, but seldom have they come up with two so far apart: one on the northern border and the other close to the southern boundary, at Penticton.

That the northern venture even flew at all in the summer of 1898 was due to the newly built telegraph line across the northern wilderness. The telegraph was a vital necessity in getting word out to the voters about what you were doing to earn their support and how well it was going. This line was started by the Collins Overland Telegraph Company, which was a subsidiary of Western Union, in 1867, part of an ill-starred intercontinental communication project. They got the wire, which was the diameter of a soda straw, as far as Hazelton, and the Dominion government then took over the line and extended it to Atlin in 1898.[21]

Considering that it took at least two weeks to reach Stewart by boat then, and an extra month to get to Teslin Lake, that wonderful wire did its duty in stalwart fashion for a politician seeking voter approval. On the other hand, the telegraph also reported the fiasco that occurred (described earlier) when the rail line that was begun up the Bear River valley out of Stewart encountered an impassable glacial barrier at Bear Pass. (Surveyors had not realized this until after they had built quite a few miles.) Turner could not survive this disclosure.[22]

An intense little man, with "a snappy walk, head erect, and body well poised," his destination when he left the premier's office was the position of agent general in London, and it was perfect for him.[23] He really excelled at promoting the province to would-be emigrants

from Britain. Beautiful colour brochures emanated from his office
showing Okanagan Lake in gorgeous Prussian blue. He successfully
worked with both the CPR and Lord Aberdeen, Canada's Governor
General and Okanagan-Valley enthusiast, to populate the Valley
in the first years of the 20th century. It was a sad day for British
Columbia when Premier McBride replaced him in London. [24]

Amid the furore of the 1898 election, McInnes seriously erred
in advising Turner that he was looking for another House leader
before it was absolutely certain that Turner lacked a majority. Turner
was furiously upset and refused to co-operate, but McInnes went
ahead and ousted him anyway. McInnes then tried to have ex-
Premier Robert Beaven take over, also without success. He settled
on Semlin, a Cariboo cattle rancher and consequently, he thought,
a man removed to a great extent from either Victoria or Vancouver
influence.

By that time political parties were forming, right, left, and centre,
informally if not in fact. Turner was from the right, and that fiery
member named Joe Martin, whom we have already met, was from
the left, and he had considerable support. Semlin tried to take the
centre path and appoint members to his cabinet from either side;
this brought on chaos in short order. This led to the departure of
Semlin and the appointment of Joe Martin, who was then quickly
deposed, and more chaos ensued. All of this of course was incredibly
damaging to McInnes, as well as to everyone else involved.

The "McInnes incident" involved the lieutenant-governor's two
sons. The first, T.R.E. McInnes, was his father's personal assistant,
and it seems he contacted Premier Turner in the middle of all this.
He offered to have his brother, W.W.B. McInnes, who was a Liberal
MP in Ottawa, guarantee Turner a majority if W.W.B. entered
B.C. politics with a seat and a cabinet post. This rather scandalous
interference into provincial politics was scornfully rejected by Turner
and was of course greatly detrimental to the lieutenant-governor
when it became known. It also led to McInnes' ouster by a faction
led by a political activist named Richard McBride. McBride and his
eastern associates prevailed on Liberal Prime Minister Sir Wilfrid
Laurier to appoint someone else to the post of Queen's representative
for the westernmost province. [25]

Finally, even though all this political infighting seems unrelated to transportation, it does indicate the mood in Victoria, and it explains why a Liberal member of Parliament from the Cariboo named Edward Gawler Prior left federal politics and entered into the provincial scene. Probably it was why he became the B.C. premier a few years later and also the chief commissioner of lands and works. Without any doubt he played a large part in Prime Minister Laurier's appointment of Sir Henri-Gustave Joly de Lotbinière, a seigneur from Quebec, to replace the beleaguered McInnes as lieutenant-governor of B.C. Lotbinière is a small town on the south bank of the St. Lawrence River about 40 miles upstream from Quebec City, and as Sir Henri had it in his surname, his ancestors at one time probably owned it. It was Lotbinière, of course, who appointed Prior to the position of B.C. premier in 1902. Prior took over from the hastily appointed James Dunsmuir—they had been desperate for a Conservative, anyone but Joe Martin!

All of this put the provincial government into disrepute and, seemingly for those who came to it from Ottawa, a certain amount of contempt. Certainly E.G. Prior seemed to think this way, although he had been an MLA in Victoria before going to Ottawa. He quickly demonstrated his disdain by his behaviour in office as first minister and as chief commissioner of lands and works. If he thought that he had carte blanche to do as he pleased because the lieutenant-governor was recommended by him, he was sadly mistaken. A fatal misunderstanding as it turned

Edward Gawler Prior, the 15th premier (November 1902 to June 1903), engineered the downfall of Lieutenant-Governor Thomas McInnes, then had another appointed who elevated him to the top provincial office. The first hardware merchant to be premier, he differed from the second, W.A.C. Bennett, in that he did not scrupulously avoid dealing with the government. He maintained that his company's bid on some bridge cables was submitted without his knowledge. No one believed him.

out—and as so often happened in those days, his downfall involved a transportation issue.

One of Prior's first moves in his new position was to favour his home territory, the Cariboo, by deciding to build a bridge across the Fraser River at Chimney Creek to replace a dangerous ferry. He instructed the department of lands and works to proceed at once. As was usually the case with longer bridges in those days, they chose to build a suspension bridge, one with iron wire cables and a wooden superstructure. They immediately advertised for tenders on the cables, and the contract for them was to be awarded by competitive bidding. There were four cables, each 2¾ inches in diameter and over 700 feet in length; not small items by any means.

The premier was also the owner of E.G. Prior and Co., a hardware company. Historian Margaret Ormsby says that Prior only saw the "informal" bids first submitted on the cables, but informal or not, he saw them. Subsequent to this a tender was submitted, by his own company, that was the lowest and that was accepted. Naturally he came under extreme censure when this became known, and his explanation that his partner did this without his knowledge was not acceptable to anyone. (It is of interest to note that the man who put the finger on him was the same Smith Curtis, MLA for Rossland, who had previously fingered Premier James Dunsmuir—strike two for his vigilance.) Prior's friend Sir Henri had no alternative than to demand his resignation, after about eight months in office. He left in June of 1903.[26]

The bridge was opened the year after that and gave good service until it was replaced in 1962. The people of the Cariboo were very lucky, because all other public-works proposals were suspended after Prior left. That Prior should return to the political scene in British Columbia as its lieutenant-governor in 1919 and stay in office until he died in 1920 is one more mystery of Ottawa politics that has puzzled historians and has never been solved.

The lieutenant-governor called on the leader of the Opposition, Richard McBride, to form a government. McBride for a number of years had been a staunch supporter of the Conservatives in eastern Canada, and was to hold office in British Columbia for the next 12½ years.

A summing-up of the first 32 years of the province, and the performance of the first 14 premiers who served it (one served twice), gives us an insight into the quirks of human nature more than anything else. To have a holder of high office who starts off by changing his name from Bill Smith to "lover of the universe," conveys a greater impression of eccentricity in a leader than could be found anywhere in the world, let alone in Canada.

His colleagues were much less colourful, but they too were eccentric in their own ways. One charged his constituents a crushing $10-a-ton tax on all freight coming from outside of their area, then wondered why they rejected him. Another gave away a large part of the foreshore on one of the world's finest harbours, based on a threat that a simple inquiry and a minute of thought would have proven to be fictitious. Then there was the one who was cut off at the pass by the tongue of a glacier. This problem simply melted away in about six decades, but the Klondike gold rushers were not about to wait.

Turner was a man who spun with the wind. First he dealt with the CPR's main competitor and awarded contracts for a railway from the Kootenays to the coast, even as the CPR built from Lethbridge along that same international border, headed for the same destination. Then a scant few years later, he reversed his position with the CPR and worked with them from his post in London to undertake one of the most successful people-moving programs ever carried out, that from Great Britain to the southern interior of B.C. He did this in the first years of the 1900s, providing a very profitable use for the CPR's ships, trains, and lake steamers. Another demonstration of his ability to quickly bury the hatchet was his sincere and complete co-operation in briefing Richard McBride after the latter had ousted him from his job in London.

All of these mostly well-meaning men battled a system of leadership that put them at the mercy of their so-called political friends. Because of this, one might forgive those who tried to line their pockets in the process or ingratiate themselves with the public, but it is hard to look kindly on the last of them. Prior totally and unashamedly abused the competitive tendering process, always a treasured safeguard throughout the years in B.C. The province had to be "a blessed land" indeed, to survive that! Both Prior and McInnes displayed a profound ignorance of the ethics of government and suffered as a result. Many years later another B.C. premier would be condemned as a result of a similar failing.

To move from the negative to the positive, there was a remarkable amount of roadwork carried through by many of these premiers to open up the province and, in the latter part of the period, to serve the new rail lines. As mentioned earlier, Premier Walkem, who became his own works commissioner, spent a lot of money on road construction, thereby putting the province seriously into debt. Despite his roads being only 7 to 10 feet wide, his mileage was impressive. In his time they continued the connection to the Cariboo Road from Savona right through to the Roman Catholic Mission by Okanagan Lake (a place now known as Kelowna), which they reached in 1876. Sadly, many sections of this early work simply disappeared quite quickly from lack of maintenance.

Premier Beaven persevered with the attempt to build a good road from Ladner to Hope, and at one time he let contracts for 100 miles of work, but the Fraser River won the day by repeatedly washing out his efforts, mostly at the upper end. From 1886 to 1891 a railway-connecting road link was rushed through from Spences Bridge to Princeton and on to Osoyoos and Penticton, but it was basically just an improved trail and did not last long, at least not throughout its full length. While premiers A.E.B. Davie and John Robson deserve credit for this, really the kudos belong to the chief commissioner of lands and works through most of their terms, a grand old B.C. pioneer cattleman, Forbes George Vernon, after whom the town of Vernon was named.

Vernon survived several premiers as commissioner of works. He started the widening of the trail from Kamloops to Vernon into a wagon road in 1876, and in the 1870s he built a trail from Fort Hope through the Coquihalla Pass to Merritt (then Nicola Forks). This route was necessary to move his and his neighbours' cattle to market from the Interior to the coast, because they could not herd them along the narrow and precipitous Cariboo Road through the Fraser Canyon. It was a good trail and a difficult one to build; cattle trails had to be at least six feet wide or the animals would scuff the edges badly when attempting to pass.

Vernon was a wonderful asset to the Interior, even if he did favour the Okanagan and its surrounding areas in his roadworks. An oil painting of Vernon graces a stairway landing in the Union Club in Victoria to this day. Few place names in B.C. are as well earned as that of Vernon.

In all honesty it should be said that the condition of these roads and trails, even when first built, was amazingly poor by present-day standards. Impassable in many places in springtime because of frost break-up and muddy and rough, bone-dry and dusty at other times, they were very infrequently maintained; when they were, it was by small crews with shovels and wheelbarrows. Many of the wagon roads lacked bridges over small creeks, and the traffic simply forded them. In forested sections large

Forbes George Vernon, B.C.'s chief commissioner of lands and works from 1876 to 1878 and from 1887 to 1895, was the genial Irish cattle rancher and politician-turned-trail-and-road-builder who built the first trail through the Coquihalla and Coldwater valleys and the first roads on the east side of the Okanagan Valley, much to the disgust of those living on the west side.

wagons quite often had trouble passing between the trees. These early road builders were not scared of distance, but their standards, resources, and equipment were pitifully inadequate.

It was little wonder that water transport was much preferred wherever rivers and lakes were available and navigable. To this end, a fleet of river and lake steamers came into being in B.C. right from the start of the province. Apart from other considerations, the politicians liked this alternative because it was fully privatized! When the railways appeared, travellers previously forced to journey by road quickly abandoned the trauma of dust-drenched or bog-hole-mired stagecoaches for the smoother and more certain movement of a train, and road travel became even more unpopular.

Let me close this chapter with an observation about the quote by Adam Smith at the beginning of it. First, we can assume that he

It was a godsend to the province that the aristocratic engineer Andrew Onderdonk of New York and San Francisco took on the challenge of building a railway through the Coast Range in 1882; such expertise was unavailable in Canada at that time. His first contract was awarded to him without tendering. On the second he was not the low bid, but when he threatened to leave, it was given to him anyway.

would probably have accepted the word "businessmen" in place of merchants. Second, when any group in control has no well-defined or positive leadership, it often reverts to the motivation of self-interest. With the deplorable lack of party discipline these premiers faced, the House virtually governed en masse, if governing it could be called. This could well have been the type of situation that Smith had in mind.

## Chapter Two

## The Railway Builder and the Debt Minders: 1903 to 1928

*"A vote against McBride's railway policy is a vote of want of confidence in British Columbia."*
—Nanaimo Free Press, 24 November, 1909

*"The PGE railway is a waif left on my doorstep. The unbuilt right-of-way in the Cariboo is a blot on the landscape."*
—Premier John Oliver, 1918

$\mathrm{T}$he official list of premiers for this period identifies their parties, an innovation begun when the party system was introduced into British Columbia. The combined terms of these 5 premiers (McBride, Bowser, Brewster, Oliver, and MacLean) was 25 years, 7 less than their 15 predecessors. (For their individual terms, see the list of premiers in Appendix B.).

On the question of whether they were collectively better at governing, it is fair to say that none of them were dismissed, except by the voters. The next-to-last premier in the above list certainly stood out, as we shall see.

As was the case with their predecessors, transportation misman- agement figured largely in this group's errors and exploitations. To the first of the group, Richard McBride, this certainly applied. For a pre- mier to stretch out his preference of one means of conveyance above all others for a period of 12½ years meant that he really worked at it—and he did. He became enraptured with railways, and he stayed that way for all of his term—not for just one railway, but for four.

The first of these was announced in 1903, the same year that McBride took office, and the proponent was the prime minister of Canada, Sir Wilfrid Laurier. The proposed rail line would come from outside of the province and be called the Grand Trunk Pacific in British Columbia. It would be an extension of the Grand Trunk Railway, which crossed Canada, and would run from Yellowhead Pass to the Pacific Ocean. The Grand Trunk, a competitor of the Canadian Northern Railway, was meant to be a second trans-Canada rail facility; neither was that yet. The Grand Trunk management was heavily populated by Americans and largely financed by them and, therefore, represented the policy of Prime Minister Laurier, which was reciprocity with the United States. Richard McBride promptly embraced the proposal and never faltered in his support of it, although he himself was a true blue Conservative and thus on the other side of the political fence from Liberal Laurier.[1]

The cost of railway construction and maintenance would weigh heavily on the financial health of British Columbia for many years to come, and it is not difficult to understand the reasons behind this financial burden. Rail lines are far better off financially if they start somewhere and end somewhere. This means that they should start at a centre of some size, preferably one that is a collection and distribution point for a large area around it, and end at a similar type of point; this assures enough through-freight and through-passenger traffic to generate revenue. Furthermore, a rail line is much more likely to be profitable if it generates what is called "way-freight" throughout its length, in other words when it picks up and drops off traffic along the way; the way-freight covers maintenance costs. Lastly, a rail line flourishes more surely when competition from other means of transportation or other rail lines is reduced.

The latter was the only advantage that Sir Wilfrid Laurier's proposal to build a rail line from Yellowhead Pass to the Pacific Ocean contained. Competition from other means of travel was non-existent, unless walking and canoeing are included. The line was to start at Yellowhead Pass, an area almost totally unpopulated. The proposed end was at an unspecified point midway along B.C.'s Pacific coast, which in 1903 was the homeland of First Nations indifferent to a railway from the rest of Canada.

It was an area only visited occasionally by outsiders, all of whom got there by sea, and those who stayed were mostly missionaries of the Church of England. Along the way the rail line would encounter very sparse human settlement consisting of villages or hamlets about 100 miles or more apart. The point was made by historian Margaret Ormsby, and no doubt it originated with pioneer school-administrator Alec Lord, that throughout its length there was not one settlement large enough to sustain a school district.

How any of this would generate any through- or way-freight at all was a valid question never gaining an answer from those asked it. The only good thing about it was that it was an interprovincial undertaking and as such, would depend on the Dominion government for regulation and assistance rather than the provincial authority. As time would tell, B.C. lawmakers nevertheless spent a great amount of the provincial treasury on it and suffered because of it almost as much as those in Ottawa.

Premier McBride did not initially display quite as much benevolence in dedicating provincial land to this railway as Premier Smithe had to the CPR, but when the facts were known, he was shown to have been almost as generous. The builders of this railway did not hold back. Their request for public land without payment was for 6 million acres, which they wanted from an almost unpopulated island (Kaien Island) alongside one of the best and largest fully sheltered harbours of the Pacific, a place now known as Prince Rupert.

Even allowing that a great part of this island was muskeg swampland, and even as anxious as he was to help out, the premier could not allow that. He did however agree to a deal for 10,000 acres of Crown land on Kaien Island, an amount exactly equal to that given up by Premier Smithe alongside Burrard Inlet. There was one additional requirement, however, no doubt to offset

During 16th premier Richard McBride's 12 years in office (January 1903 to December 1915), he supported four railways, emptying the provincial treasury in the process and ending up with a $10 million deficit. To railway promoters Mackenzie and Mann, he was like a sitting duck ready to be fleeced, and that they did, to the dismay of Finance Minister R.G. Tatlow.

the criticism that Smithe encountered—the premier demanded a payment of $1 an acre, $10,000 in all.

Now follows a very strange series of events in which the bright halo of rectitude surrounding Premier McBride in this transaction dims considerably. The $10,000 was not paid to the provincial government by the Grand Trunk Pacific Railway, but by one of their contractors, a man who then received the title. This individual is said to have subsequently handed that title over to the GTP for what was said to have been the same payment, but not before he lavished a large payment of money to a Victoria lawyer in the course of the transaction, apparently in respect of undetermined services. The government finally received $2.50 per acre for the land on Kaien Island.[2]

This should have gone to a public inquiry for several reasons. First, the province should never have handed over this land to an individual, since it was a donation to a facility of expected benefit to the public.

Second, the Victoria lawyer should have been required to reveal the nature of the services he had performed for this remuneration. Rumour said the lawyer facilitated some highly profitable land deals for the contractor in the area. No such inquiry took place to clear the air, which remained murky as Premier McBride lost a good man from his cabinet, something that was to occur quite repeatedly during his term of office. The rage of the Boer War veterans who had been promised land in that area was sufficient for a head to roll in cabinet, but it was not that of McBride.

Robert Francis Green, the province's chief commissioner of lands and works from 1903 to 1906, was a native of Peterborough, Ontario, and a veteran of the Riel Rebellion. After serving as the mayor of Kaslo, B.C., he was elected to the legislative assembly in 1898. He was the sacrificial lamb for the Kaien Island railway-land scandal in Premier McBride's administration. He ran for Parliament in 1912 with success and was finally appointed to the Senate.

The man to go was the chief commissioner of lands and works Robert Francis Green, who had quite recently taken over this position from the premier. (A list of chief commissioners of lands and works, ministers of public works and highways, etc., is included in Appendix B.) Green was a former mayor of Kaslo, B.C., and he was proving to be an excellent chief commissioner. He had already challenged the powers of the public-works superintendents throughout the province, whose functions were much more political than administrative; they handled the greatest share of patronage appointments for the more remote areas. Green was also fully in favour of equipping the workforce on the roads with more than hand shovels and wheelbarrows, an intervention strongly resisted by those superintendents. He also put out a very strong message to them to raise the standard of work done on the roads, which was extremely poor.[3]

The question remains as to whether Green deserved to take the rap for this, or whether McBride used him as a convenient scapegoat to deflect the searchlight from himself. We will never know the answer to that, but both McBride and Green were eventually declared to be quite blameless in the whole matter. It seems unlikely indeed that an experienced politician as was Green would have engaged in the actions he was accused of without McBride's knowledge. The sacrificial lamb landed on his feet in national politics, probably due to his party loyalty. He gained a seat in Parliament in Ottawa and eventually became a Senator.[4]

As could be expected, the power behind the Grand Trunk Pacific Railway was mostly wielded by one man. In keeping with Prime Minister Laurier's policy of full reciprocity with the United States, and the dominance of Americans in the railways of North America in these years, it is not surprising that that man was American. His name was Charles Melville Hays, and while Van Horne was said to be forceful as a chief executive officer, Hays was the same way in that role, but he achieved it less visibly. To the accusation that he was building a railway to nowhere, he had a ready answer—"I am going to make it somewhere!"—and the metropolis he envisaged on the Pacific coast was eventually the city of Prince Rupert.

Later he undertook the same task at the eastern end, creating the city of Prince George at the confluence of the Fraser and Nechako rivers. One of Hays' bargaining levers to get land was Premier McBride's desire for construction to begin at Prince Rupert and make its way eastwards, rather than for it to start at Yellowhead Pass. That would have meant using supplies from Alberta, which would have saved a great deal of money for the railway builders.[5]

To assure that his coastal city had suitable stature, Hays took action in his usual highly competent style as early as 1906. He hired Francis Mawson Rattenbury, the noted architect who had just completed the Empress Hotel in Victoria, to produce a railway hotel in Prince Rupert for the GTP that would surpass in its magnificence all others owned by the CPR. Rattenbury worked on it off and on until the spring of 1912, when his sponsor tragically left the scene. Charles Hays went to the bottom of the Atlantic Ocean with the RMS *Titanic* on his way back from a money-raising trip to Europe.[6]

Despite this body blow from which it never really recovered, the railway was completed in 1914, the same year that the world war started that would assure its bankruptcy. By supreme irony, it reached that sad state a few years later on the same day that the city by the sea, without a huge hotel, did. Finally going somewhere and coming from somewhere, the GTP did it with nothing in between, and that hard economic fact secured its demise, one that was only delayed for some years, at the expense of the taxpayer. This was the same fate to be met by all four of the railways McBride supported. The Yellowhead-to-Prince Rupert rail line was eventually reduced to the status of a spur line until the Second World War gave it a boost. After that the advent of unit coal trains revived it (unit trains are very large, up to a hundred cars, and carry one commodity only—in this case, coal being exported to Japan).

The next of these rail lines of uncertain destiny came to pass as a result of the first. Short-sightedness in the assessment of rail transport's viability was endemic in those days. When the Grand Trunk Pacific was announced, the people of the Lower Mainland demonstrated this quality. About the only hard fact supporting the building of the GTP was that Prince Rupert was several hundred miles closer to far eastern markets by sea than was Vancouver, and trans-Pacific maritime trade was slowly developing out of that seaport. They saw the development of a railway to Prince Rupert, and the development of that port city, as a threat. It was one that never came to pass, but in that era of limitless horizons it seemed ominous indeed.

Four interested ears heard this, and in no time at all the owners of them were knocking on Premier McBride's door in Victoria. Why not counter the concerns of these people in the south by building yet another rail line to Vancouver? Twice the capacity to move export materials to the Lower Mainland would certainly offset this northern challenge. Only two men in Canada could assure this outcome along with the added advantage of making it an all-Canadian undertaking— William Mackenzie and Donald Mann were these men of course. Like Premier Turner before him, McBride took the bait, and with Laurier's support, yet another trans-provincial line was under way. As with the line in the north, McBride never wavered in his support.

Railway building had become his *raison d'être*, and he never lost his love for it. McBride's investment of provincial funds with these two brash railway builders was to be substantial.[7]

Late in 1909 McBride suddenly called an election. The next day he announced that he had signed an agreement with Donald Mann for the construction of 600 miles of railway from Yellowhead Pass to Vancouver and that the province had guaranteed the interest on a loan up to $21 million, or $35,000 per mile.[8]

Once again a McBride railway adventure brought reaction, and in this case two of his best cabinet ministers left him. The first was Robert Garnet Tatlow, a Vancouver businessman and a very fine minister of finance. He had succeeded Green in lands and works, and he had totally overhauled its financial management; after that, he had taken over the finance department in the reorganization. Well in advance of that, he had warned McBride not to contemplate any investment at all of provincial funds with Mackenzie and Mann. He said they did not need it, even if their proposal was approved by Ottawa, and he urged that there be no provincial funding whatsoever. When the premier ignored his advice, Tatlow left. His desertion severely diminished McBride's stature with the business establishment, but there was more to come.

Frederick John Fulton was a very competent lawyer of high principles and keen intellect and a valued member of McBride's cabinet. He hailed from Kamloops and was the member for that constituency. He took over lands and works from Tatlow and undertook some much-needed legal work revising the statutes to make the new government structure of ministries effective. As part of this, he drew up the first Highway Act, which from then on was one of the most successful Acts on the books in Victoria. Fulton's one aim in life as the member for Kamloops was the restoration of the Fraser Canyon road link from the Lower Mainland to his home town. It had been totally destroyed by the building of the CPR main line in the mid-1880s.

Fulton had enthusiastically supported the new department of public works as it conducted surveys to replace the old Royal Engineer's road and threaded a line for it from Yale to Spuzzum, above and below the CPR line, with the greatest of difficulty. They were almost ready to start work when McBride dropped the bombshell that there was to be a second railway in the Canyon; any hope of replacing the historic road disappeared at once. In 1909 they lacked the resources and the machinery necessary to take on the job of making room for two rail lines and a roadway in that precipitous, steep, and dangerous canyon. Fulton's dream of regaining a road went out the cabinet chamber window, and as Mackenzie and Mann clinched their deal, he followed it. Sadly, the public was led to an unlikely assumption that Fulton and Tatlow had resigned over their allegiance to the CPR, Fulton having been a lawyer for them and Tatlow an accountant. All of this happened in 1909, and after it McBride was left with only one of his ministers as a close associate, his dear friend and attorney general, another brilliant lawyer by the name of William John (Bill) Bowser. (There will be more on him later.)

When McBride assumed the premiership, he found that the spinning door to his office had sucked all the money out of it. He immediately shut down all new roadwork, but of course he had to finish that which was already started, and this included the Chimney Creek bridge. It was just one of a number of road projects started by the man before him, Edward Prior, leaving an empty cashbox. This seemed to sour McBride on all public-works expenditure of any kind, an attitude not lessened by his concentration on railways being built by others.

Reality came back to bite him quite suddenly, however, when his actions in 1909 set back any hope of a road link to the coast. Another player had just entered into the transportation scene by that year, and its curve of acceptance was rising exponentially. This was the automobile, and the wealthy and powerful men in Vancouver and Victoria had quickly taken a liking to it, as had many of their kind in the hinterland and in the adjoining provinces. The problem was that British Columbia had very little in the way of acceptable roads to indulge this new distraction, especially between the regions, and nothing at all if you wanted to drive eastwards from the coast or westwards towards it from the interior of the province or from the rest of Canada.

It was really little wonder that Fred Fulton had resigned when his dream of driving in an automobile from the coast to his constituency disappeared like the remains of the first Alexandra Bridge. That bridge was tipped over when its foundations were displaced by the 1894 flood. The cables holding it up were finally cut around that time, because the railway builders were told in a letter from the deputy minister of public works that the province had no further need of that bridge or that road. This was virtually an assertion that no roadway at all was needed between B.C.'s coast and its southern interior, one of the most questionable statements ever made by a B.C. civil servant about a transportation issue.

McBride immediately had to seek out another way by which automobiles could move from the Lower Mainland to the Interior other than on railway flatcars. The logical way for that would have been by converting to a road the long-established trail built by Edgar Dewdney and the Royal Engineers from Hope to Princeton. That he did not take this route brings yet another railway into this mishmash.

As mentioned earlier, ever since the start of the century the Vancouver business establishment had desperately sought a way to benefit from the mining boom in the Boundary and Kootenay districts. They centered on a coast-to-Kootenay rail link, and this was almost in sight in 1909. The Great Northern Railway, under its energetic President Jim Hill, was busily building and planning its line from the Boundary District westwards towards Vancouver, its final entry into B.C. coming at Nighthawk just west of Osoyoos. It had reached Princeton and was fully occupying the Tulameen valley, running north and west of there with railway construction in 1909. That was the year Hill announced that he had filed plans with the board of railway commissioners in Ottawa for a line through Coquihalla Pass and that his proposed line had been accepted.[9]

This was very bad news for the CPR, and particularly the planners of its offshoot, the Kettle Valley Railway, who were also working on a line from the Boundary District to Vancouver, but had not yet lodged their claim to the Pass. They were thus effectively stymied by their overbearing competitor for a route to Hope from Princeton, either by the Tulameen valley or by the Coquihalla valley. To add to their misery, it was well known at that time that the B.C. department of public works was planning a road from Hope to Princeton through Allison Pass, which would eliminate their remaining alternative. No one believed that it would be easy for a road and a railway to be built together along Skagit Bluffs.

It seems almost certain that the Canadian railwaymen approached Premier McBride and suggested to him that he find another way for the road. This was the only conceivable reason that a Vancouver consulting engineer, A.E. Cleveland, would have announced that the proposed road he had been hired to survey would go from Hope to Princeton via the Silverhope Creek valley and Gibson Pass, rather than by Allison Pass. The Gibson Pass route was eight miles longer, and it ran along the base of the highest peaks in the Cascades (the last part of the Skagit Range, holding the remnant of glaciation), and this shielded the Allison Pass route from heavy winter snowfall. The existing rough trail up the Silverhope Valley was notorious for avalanches, rock slides, and torrents of debris because the mountains beside it were the first barriers encountered by Pacific storms flowing in up the Fraser Valley. In addition, the Allison Pass route in 1909 had 29 miles of wagon road already built on it.[10]

Started before the First World War, the Gibson Pass road was abandoned at the war's end with less than half of its mileage roughed out; it was never continued. The Kettle Valley Railway eventually shared the Coquihalla Pass with the Great Northern. All that Premier McBride achieved by his concessions to the railways in all of this was a most damaging delay to the building of a much-needed road link from Hope to Princeton. The construction of the Hope-Princeton Highway, largely due to this, was not achieved until 40 years later.

If the good citizens of the most westerly province could offer no thanks to "good old Dick" for this, they could muster even less for his final adventure into railways. He was a sitting duck to the good people of Squamish, a little-used port on Howe Sound, in their bid to have the town be the terminus for a railway from the interior of the province. After all, why should those people in Vancouver, Prince Rupert, and Stewart have all the fun? Granted, Stewart's had been short-lived, but it had been great while it lasted. McBride bought it all again, and he invested heavily in provincial funding to support it, because this one, the Pacific Great Eastern (PGE), was all within the province.

Premier McBride had just won an election in 1909 by a large majority, and the sky was truly the limit for his railway assemblage for at least the next three years. He won another election in 1912, once more with a good majority. During this election, McBride's supporters even made a promise on his behalf for an all-rail connection to Vancouver Island by means of a bridge over Seymour Narrows.[11]

There was little doubt that the "please go easy" line, the PGE, went from nowhere to nowhere, especially at its northern end, where it went nowhere at all for the next 40 years. When McBride left office in 1915, it had reached the small Cariboo road community of Clinton, after struggling through some of the steepest ravines and lakeshores in the coast range. All that McBride's celebrated railway policy brought for Premier John Oliver was trouble, including a $10-million deficit and a totally unauthorized advance of $7 million from the province to the PGE to go with guarantees to other railways totalling $80 million.[12]

McBride's follies were expensive. If ever the harm from his love for railways took material form, it was in the Hells Gate slide of 1913, an event that severely restricted the flow of the Fraser River. The slide was triggered by his railway builders, Mackenzie and Mann, and brought lengthy hardship to the fishing industry in B.C.[13] An Ottawa fishing commissioner described the Fraser River fishery in 1920 as "a monumental record of man's folly and greed." This unkind comment could be viewed as a description of much of McBride's career, which he ended by resigning. Leaving the turmoil of his last months as premier, he worked for several years as the agent general for B.C. in London.

He worked hard there for Canadians in the First World War until his death in 1917 of Bright's Disease at the age of 48. This happened on the eve of his return to Canada, a tragic ending for a man who gave much to his province and his country. He was doubtless heartened, shortly before he was to leave Britain, by a letter from a British member of Parliament. This man, who was an investor in B.C., told him that the hearts of the people were with him and his railway policy right to the end of his term as premier, which was true. That this British MP was also the owner of a fish cannery at Prince Rupert was only barely relevant.

As "the people's Dick" (as he was affectionately known) did not depart with an election, it was necessary for his party to name a successor. This turned out to be William John Bowser, his attorney general and his only close associate remaining in cabinet. Bowser took over in December 1915 and lasted exactly 11 months in the office. He had come into the premiership with a cloud over his head, one in addition to that of a world war, which had darkened the sky for McBride.

This cloud on British Columbia's horizon was a long-lasting one for the province; it was the Pacific Great Eastern Railway. Bowser had supported McBride's devotion to the Canadian Northern Pacific Railway (as Mackenzie and Mann's line through the Fraser Canyon was first called, although it soon dropped the

William J. Bowser became 17th premier (December 1915 to November 1916) at a difficult time. He might have been re-elected but for two mistakes. First, he should never have interceded for the PGE when he was attorney general, and second, he should not have called out the army for a lengthy stay to quell the miners of Vancouver Island—there had to have been a better way.

Frederick John Fulton, chief commissioner of lands and works from 1907 to 1908, was a highly respected lawyer in Kamloops before representing it in the legislature. He reorganized lands and works in the legal sense, drafting a Highway Act that has served well ever since. He resigned because he got another railway to his constituency, not a road.

"Pacific."), and he was even more enthusiastic about the one that kept that word in its name.

Rather unfortunately, Bowser had not only supported the PGE, he had actively promoted it to then-Premier McBride. He did this while still retained as the lawyer for the railway after he became attorney general. This was a case of the highest officer of the court also acting as a lobbyist to it. Even in those days, many British Columbians found that hard to stomach, even as their digestive systems were struggling with that particular railway, which was in time popularly dubbed "Prince George Eventually."

Sir William Mackenzie (left) and Sir Donald Mann (right), were Canada's greatest railway promoters.

In 1915, McBride's last year, everything in B.C. had started to unravel, mostly because of the sudden withdrawal, due to the war, of the massive British investment made in the province. Desperate for something to promise, McBride had finally started to talk about extending a bad thing even further—the PGE to Alaska! Even his closest Conservative supporters decided that this was too much; this was part of a general disillusionment with him that was the root cause for his departure. His opponents described his lasting monuments in the province as "the railways of steal," mostly because of the rumours that PGE funds went into the Conservative campaign budgets.[14]

Bill Bowser, his successor who in many ways had been the power behind the throne for the Conservatives, was quite capable of carrying on. He could have been a fine premier for many years, but that was not to be. He demonstrated his capability early on by making some excellent ministerial appointments, several of which required by-elections; in all of these, the appointees were defeated. The writing was on the wall, and in the election of November 1916, the Liberals took power. What was Bowser's mistake? Well, it was not just favouring the PGE, an error that McBride shared; it was how he did it that distinguished him!

The new Liberal premier, Harlan Carey Brewster, was seemingly fated to have his name either prefixed by "fish canner," which he was, or by "the gatherer of wormwood and rue." The latter

Harlan Carey Brewster, B.C.'s 18th premier (November 1916 to March 1918) left Ottawa with an agreement for road funding that required future roadwork to be overseen by professional engineers. He never saw it come to pass, because he died of pneumonia on the way home.

was no doubt a suitable tag for a premier whose term in office almost completely fell within the years most noted for the province's youth dying by the thousands on the Western Front. Before the war ended, Harlan Brewster also died, in a Calgary hospital in March of 1918, from a bout of pneumonia incurred on his return journey from Ottawa, where he had gone to discuss post-war reconstruction. At that meeting he had signed an agreement, one condition of which was to have great impact on the future of roads administration of the province.

Brewster was notable in that he appointed three future premiers of B.C. to his cabinet—John Oliver, John Duncan MacLean, and Thomas Dufferin Pattullo— as, respectively, minister of agriculture and railways, provincial secretary, and minister of lands. He also appointed a medical doctor as his first minister of public works. While this added a flavour of professionalism, seemingly a new priority, it

The province's 19th premier, John Oliver (March 1918 to August 1927), decided in 1924 to replace the road between Yale and Spences Bridge. He made one serious error: He was offered financial assistance for this project by the federal government, but turned it down in favour of collecting tolls. Before the job was finished in 1927, he knew the tolls would never pay for the costs involved. The tolls remained in effect for 20 years.

flew in the face of the long-held notion that medical men make poor administrators. Dr. James Horace King, who served from 1916 to 1922, was an excellent minister of public works, as was his successor in the job from 1922 to 1928, another medical man, Dr. Henry William Sutherland.

There was one outstanding feature of the post-war reconstruction agreement with the Dominion government signed by Harlan Brewster in 1918 that was of much significance to the public works department. It was a proviso that no funding from the senior government was to be expended on public works unless it was administered by a professional engineer. From this, it was concluded by Brewster's successor, Premier John Oliver, that forthwith all the road superintendents in British Columbia were to be replaced by district engineers. To guess why the national government included this condition, we must consider a phenomenon that had increasingly intruded upon the public service in Canada, particularly in the first decades of the 1900s: the problem of patronage, or otherwise stated, the bestowal of favours (financial or otherwise) on the party faithful.

This problem cropped up in the department of lands and works from the very beginning of the provincial form of government. Its source was the system of land settlement by the process known as pre-emption, which involved granting a tract of Crown land to the settler without payment, but with certain obligations. To the settler's promise to improve that land was added the duty to assist in providing access to it by a road and sometimes the added responsibility of

Dr. James Horace King, minister of public works from 1916 to 1922, served under premiers Brewster and Oliver. Later, he became the federal minister of health for the Liberals. While in Ottawa, he greatly helped his East Kootenays constituency by obtaining Dominion government assistance to build a tourist road from Cranbrook to Vermilion Pass; it became the best paved highway in B.C.

Dr. Henry William Sutherland, minister of public works from 1922 to 1926, was a country doctor from the Cariboo. He oversaw the restoration of the Fraser Canyon road under premiers Oliver and MacLean and suffered the embarrassment of having to cancel a national meeting of the Good Roads Society in celebration of its opening, because the road was not yet ready.

contributing to the extension of that road to the lands beyond it. In this way, the proper overall settlement of the area with adequate road access could be assured.

As well as this, grants were made to the various ridings for road construction or improvement at the request of their member of the legislature. Because civil-service road workers in those days were typically fully engaged in maintenance duties, especially on bridges, the settlers often ended up doing the work themselves, paid or unpaid, usually after a foreman was elected to supervise. When the Depression of the 1930s set in, it was necessary to find another way in addition to this pre-emption roadwork to help most farmers pay their taxes when produce prices took a dive. This was why a process was set up for them to work off taxes by doing roadwork. [15]

A typical centre with a large number of small- to medium-sized farming operations was the Creston Valley, and the program for working off taxes there was extensive, lasting right into the 1950s. Farm tractors towing trailers would appear every day in the spring and summer in preparation for work on the area's roads. Work was seldom done in the fall, because they were harvesting then. In the spring, if there was a bad breakup and frost damage on the roads, these tractors were sometimes put to work helping traffic through the mudholes. The road superintendents had to be careful about this, however; some of the farmers would haul water to the road in the hours of darkness to keep a good thing going! This tax-relief work was finally stopped due to such complications as the Workers Compensation Act and its safety regulations; the farmers were just not safe enough at work on the roads. Unfortunately, the tax-relief project had been a good avenue for patronage under the Liberals and under the Conservatives before them. It also went on under the Coalition government that headed the province from 1941 to 1952.

It should be noted that the overall supervision of the process, including the vetting of the foremen appointed as politically acceptable, was the function of the road superintendent of the riding concerned. The road superintendent's areas coincided with ridings, a very unwise mating of politics and road management. That explains the concern of Robert Green, Premier McBride's chief commissioner of lands and works, when he set about improving the efficiency of the road superintendents in his department.

Unfortunately, Green left quite soon. His successors, particularly the first minister of public works under McBride, a man nicknamed Thomas "Good Roads" Taylor, tried to right things, but was not successful. It was left to the new district engineers under Premier Oliver and his public works minister, Dr. King, to take up the banner and meet patronage and special privilege head-on. Unfortunately they did not clean the decks completely, although they tried—John Oliver did not gain his nickname "Honest John" without good reason.

When the district engineers took over, the road superintendents either took early retirement or were demoted to senior foremen. They then watched, probably with some amusement, the green engineers

Thomas "Good Roads" Taylor was the first minister of public works (1908 to 1914) after the term "minister" came into use in 1908 and the department was separated from that of lands and works. The first cabinet minister to use an automobile, he lost his Revelstoke seat when he built a trans-provincial road in the south instead of rebuilding through the Fraser Canyon. He was another sacrificial lamb for Premier McBride.

take on the many problems of politics. As they knew, and as soon became evident, the truth of the matter was that politicians would never divorce themselves from roads in British Columbia, and road engineers there would never be rid of political interference. This point was seemingly lost on Premier Oliver, whose instructions to his new engineers were that they should not concern themselves with politics. He did, however, cover himself somewhat by adding that they should always have a clear and practical reason for their actions.[16]

Oliver had been the minister of agriculture and railways under Brewster, and when he became premier, he attributed most of the $18 million deficit facing the province to that Coast-to-Cariboo rail link. He stated emphatically that he wanted nothing to do with it. "It is a waif on our doorstep," he declared, "and the unbuilt right-of-way in the Cariboo is like an unkempt, undrained blot on the landscape." Nonetheless, he had to stay with it, and rail was laid to Clinton.[17]

The experience with the PGE soured Oliver on all public works projects in his first months as premier, a view shared by international bondsmen immediately after the war, who forbade B.C. to undertake any public works for several years because of its accumulated debt load. Of course this debt load had been mostly incurred by McBride on railways. However, the demand by returned servicemen for land brought an accompanying need for roads, and in a few years Oliver conceived and executed an excellent road program, mostly in the southern Interior. He also achieved the landmark road connection through the Fraser and Thompson canyons between Yale and Spences Bridge.

It was to Oliver's second minister of public works, Dr. Henry William Sutherland of the Cariboo riding, that the honour (or burden) of calling the road contracts in the canyons fell. In September 1924 three contracts for the replacement of the roadway in the Fraser and Thompson canyons were called. To emphasize the new climate of openness that Premier Oliver demanded, it was announced that the contracts would be examined and let by the members of the legislature in session, not by the public works department. This was an innovation that was carried out on this project but never repeated.[18]

While machinery had improved by 1924, the task of replacing this road alongside the railways was still a gamble. Pneumatic tires for trucks did not arrive until 1926, as did antifreeze. Steam shovels were used for the most part to load wagons pulled by mules or horses, and grading was in many cases done by horse-drawn pull graders, although there were some tractors. One subcontractor at the Tilton Creek section was recommended because of the excellence of his stock, i.e., his animals. The first contract, the one most feared, was for 13.5 miles between Yale and the Alexandra Bridge; it was done on time. It was the second and third, 24 miles each, from Spuzzum to Boothroyd and from Lytton to Spences Bridge, that gave them trouble. (Boothroyd to Lytton was done by the government.) The Spuzzum-to-Boothroyd section was done in reasonable time but nonetheless cost twice the estimate. The contract for Lytton to Spences Bridge was awarded in 1924, but the government would not let the successful contractor begin work before early 1926.

The delay was seemingly due to design flaws, and an elaborate Canadian Good Roads Association opening had to be cancelled because of it. Extras on this contract put the final cost at three and a half times the original bid when it was completed in 1927. The only comment that the deputy minister of public works had about it all was that he spent most of his time finding summer jobs on it for the sons of Victoria politicians and senior civil servants. The final product was very narrow, in some places two feet narrower than its predecessor, but it was noted for the excellence of its rock walls, which replaced most of the grasshopper trestles and the very dangerous timber cribbings put there by the Royal Engineers. The Alexandra Bridge was replaced.

Oliver also took over the building of the road over the Monashee Pass from Vernon to Nakusp. This had been started by German prisoners during the war; a clue that patronage still remained under Honest John was that the same contractor won repeated contracts, one each year from 1922 to 1925, to rebuild it, all without competitive bidding.[19]

Oliver's big mistake was that he did not solve the problem of patronage sufficiently to at least appear to be doing something. The situation worsened with time, as fewer voters benefited from it than did not. He died of cancer in August 1927 and was replaced by his provincial secretary, John Duncan MacLean, who served until the election of July 1928.

John Oliver was a tragic figure, and it was almost a blessing that this honest and well-meaning man died before he saw his party go down to a rather stunning defeat to the Conservatives, who got 35 seats to the Liberals' 12. Bowed down by the provincial debt left to him by his predecessor, he suffered grievously from the irresponsibility of his own party members and their actions, exploiting their period in power, that were so much in contrast to his own. But no one ever said that politics is fair.

Looking at all the premiers to hold that position in B.C.'s history up to this time, it is difficult to overlook a comment made publicly by the feisty old B.C. officeholder, Gilbert Martin Sproat. He came to B.C in 1860, returned to England in 1865, and five years later became the first agent general for B.C. in London. He came back to Canada in 1876 and soon become Indian land commissioner and then the gold commissioner in the Kootenays. Sproat thereby knew the men in charge of the province right from its inception.

When he heard in 1912 that the deputy minister of public works had told the chief engineer of the Canadian Northern Railway that the province had no further use for a road through the Fraser Canyon, it was too much. His scornful description of those in charge obviously went back right to the beginning, "a civil service queerly recruited and commanded by a group of piddling Premiers," he said.[20]

It is notable that he said this before the advent of Bill Bowser and John Oliver, and it is unlikely that they would have earned his scorn to this extent. But as for the others, they certainly were not memorable for their leadership because the system bred expediency rather than statesmanship, a distinction that few premiers were able to make.

# Chapter Three

# Partisan Politics Finally Coalesce: 1928 to 1952

*"The annual budget of the provincial government should be reduced from $25 million to $6 million."*

*"The present government should form a coalition with the Liberals for the next election."*
—The Kidd Committee, a group initiated by H.R. MacMillan and commissioned by the one-term government of Premier Simon Fraser Tolmie, 1929

*"Under no circumstances will British Columbia consent to Dominion control over Provincial expenditures."*
—Premier T.D. Pattullo, May 1934

In 1928 and for the first 10 months of 1929 British Columbia enjoyed unprecedented prosperity. There were reported to be 83 millionaires among the Vancouver business community, that lump-like force in the provincial economy, all profiting mightily from its fish, lumber, and minerals, seemingly endless resources there for the taking.[1] Most of them were riding high as they traded in the stock exchange, a rather frantic money-multiplying sideline—at least it was up until October 29, 1929, Black Thursday, when it all collapsed.

Simon Fraser Tolmie, the 21st premier (August 1928 to November 1933), was in the wrong place at the wrong time. Too nice in his thought and manner, as a Conservative he should never have been premier when the stock market collapsed; it was all too much for him. As a veterinarian, he should have known that if you let a sleeping dog lie too long, it will rise up and bite you. That is what he did with the Kidd Committee report. He let it lie and it bit hard.

The election of July 1928 had seen a native son of B.C. appointed premier. Simon Fraser Tolmie was the offspring of parents from prominent families at the top of the Hudson's Bay Company hierarchy. His mother was Jane Work, the daughter of Chief Factor John Work, and his father was Chief Factor Dr. William Fraser Tolmie. A Conservative politician from Saanich, outside of Victoria, and a member of Parliament in Ottawa since 1917, Simon Tolmie had served in two Conservative cabinets and was once the minister of agriculture (a rather sensible post for a veterinarian). He became leader of the Conservative Party in B.C. in 1926. Not relishing a return to the farmyard, he had stayed on in the east for two years while waiting for the call to lead the party in the election that was impatiently hoped for as Oliver's popularity faltered and, after Oliver had died, as the lacklustre MacLean held on.

When that election was finally announced in the summer of 1928, Tolmie resigned his post and his seat in Parliament and headed back west. On his arrival he triumphantly toured B.C. by automobile, introducing himself to the people of his party in the hinterland. No doubt he had heard of the Liberals' road patronage as he covered over 4,000 miles of the roads they had tended before he entered on the campaign to render those responsible unemployed. This objective was very successfully achieved by him and his party and was possibly the only success they had.[2]

Two qualities were necessary to a political leader in the West in those days: the killer instinct and the ability to lead. Most of B.C.'s premiers since its inclusion in Canada had demonstrated at

Nelson Seymour Lougheed, minister of public works from 1928 to 1929, did what no minister in charge of roads should ever do: He promised he would start on a road connection the following summer and finish it in the following two or three years. The collapse of Wall Street that fall meant that the Tolmie government had no funds at all for road building before they left office in 1933. This ill-timed promise plagued the incoming premier, T.D. Pattullo, until 1939, when he could thankfully say that nothing would be done until the war was over.

least one of these, and with a bit of luck, that had been enough to see them through. Simon Fraser Tolmie did not demonstrate either, nor did he enjoy any luck at all in his time as first minister.

The first indication that this gentle, likeable man lacked the killer instinct involved his first minister of public works, Nelson Seymour Lougheed. His only road-building season in a prosperous province was in 1929. From the fiscal years 1928-29 and 1929-30, the expenditure for road improvement in the Dewdney District, Lougheed's riding, rose from $298,000 to $928,000—this from a roads budget of less than $4 million for the whole province. As Premier Tolmie soon found out, nothing is more likely to arouse the ire of voters from the Interior than a government led by a coastal premier spending more than a quarter of its road funds in a coastal riding. The Dewdney road, on which it was all spent, was very soon renamed the Lougheed Highway, a title it holds to this day. That this work was only mentioned indirectly and the road not named in the chief engineer's report for 1929, tells us something of Lougheed. Tolmie was forced to make a cabinet change, and Rolf Bruhn, a man from Salmon Arm, took over public works.[3]

When the stock market crash suddenly put the corporate earnings of the Lower Mainland industry leaders onto a steep downward slope matched only by the decline of provincial revenues, the Vancouver business community promptly went into a state of complete panic. A delegation to Victoria led by lumber baron H.R. MacMillan resulted in a committee formed among them to recommend action in the emergency. This group, called the Kidd Committee after its leader, George Kidd, was granted access to all provincial government records and given all civil-service help possible to assist them in their task. In April of 1932, after an unrecorded deliberation, they came up with an incredible recommendation: They proposed a drastic cut in the provincial government's annual budget from $25 million to $6 million! To add to the agony, they also advocated a similarly drastic decrease in the province's relief payments to the unemployed—this during a crisis in which one person out of eight of the workforce was on relief, with that number steadily rising. Finally, they recommended the closing of the PGE Railway, one of the very few acceptable proposals they made. As a further indication of the depth of the crisis, the value of building permits issued in Vancouver went from $22 million in 1929 to $2 million in 1934, a drop equalled only between 1913 and 1917, when they went from $20 million to $1 million.[4]

At this point, the premier should have stepped in and refused to accept this recommendation; he should have shaken up the committee and called upon all levels of society to work out a joint approach to the problems. Instead, he did nothing. He just let it sit there for six months with orders that it be kept secret. Of course, it leaked out and its insensitivity destroyed him. The committee stayed on with all of its powers intact, eventually renaming itself the "Economy Committee." A reading of the Nelson public-works district files of the 1930s shows a relentless, continuing reduction in the number of staff working on the roads and in the salaries of those who remained. To add to the workers' misery, the committee constantly requested information and endless statistics and acted most unpleasantly. People will do that when they have unlimited authority over something for which they have no responsibility.

The excerpt from the department of public works' annual reports reproduced at the end of this chapter shows details of the relief roadwork program. The problems of running a road-maintenance and construction organization under such conditions can hardly be imagined. Certainly it was to be expected that the stunned public would disapprove of a party representing the more wealthy side of society. The Conservatives were simply there at the wrong time.

When the five-year mandatory period for another election came around in the fall of 1933, it is little wonder that the voters rejected Tolmie. He lost all seats but one, including his own. The district engineers, who had watched in wonder as their local Liberal-appointed road foremen departed five years earlier and were replaced by Conservative supporters, were fated to watch this transpire once again but in reverse, as the Liberals returned. They must have felt some amusement when they recalled Premier Oliver's remarks that they should not concern themselves with politics.

Tolmie's foremost error was to let a Vancouver power group run his government into the ground. Not unexpectedly, considering the history of premiers so far, his final agony was linked to a transportation issue—the building and maintaining of British Columbia's roads, which by then seriously needed attention. Patronage, as usual, was a factor in the demise of those who invoked it. Nonetheless, the collapse of the stock markets must take the lion's share of the blame. Poet W.H. Auden described the 1930s as the low, dishonest decade, and it was indeed.

If Simon Tolmie found a difficult situation when he took up the reins in 1928, it was nothing compared to the mess that Thomas Dufferin Pattullo faced when he became premier in November 1933. When the new year dawned, it was not long before the disaster in the economy was exacerbated by a naturally caused one in the Fraser Valley, where heavy winter snow led to widespread flooding in the spring.

Pattullo had been the minister of lands under Oliver, and after that he was a very efficient leader of the Opposition. He needed

Thomas Dufferin (Duff) Pattullo, the 22nd premier (November 1933 to December 1941), had Scottish roots and an un-Scottish last name. He was lured westwards by Klondike gold, then by the bright prospects of Prince Rupert, but he found the end of his rainbow in politics. Darkened by the Great Depression, his political career outlived that but not his Liberal colleagues. A stalwart supporter of the common man, he got no credit for this virtue, or for the bridge bearing his name.

all the efficiency he could find in his new job, and the consensus of opinion was that he provided it. After all, he had been to the Klondike, and he had served on the Dawson City council before moving to Prince Rupert to sell real estate and, in the course of time, becoming the representative in Victoria of these hardy rain-swept citizens. So he, unlike Tolmie, knew something of how people think outside the southwest corner of the province. He appointed Frank Mitchell MacPherson, a seasoned politician from Grand Forks, to be the minister of public works. MacPherson's strongest point was that he was not noted publicly for anything, but there is no doubt that he worked constantly behind the scenes for the party. His backroom dealings were to spell trouble for Pattullo.

As described in the detail of the relief roadwork, Tolmie had endured the setting-up of the relief camps, after a scheme to hire the unemployed province-wide had broken the bank. Then he had suffered the indignity of an Ottawa bureaucracy running his road department, but only for six months; Pattullo had to put up with it for three years. The annual reports did not record the agony, despair, anger, and frustration of almost everybody in British Columbia concerning the downward plunge in their everyday life. Some people floated above it, but very few. The anger of the district engineers about army engineers directing work on their roads and using their equipment was matched only by the frustration of these military men at having, as the report to the minister of public works for the

It was well known that in the '30s, and for some decades after that, party membership in B.C. sometimes carried benefits to the faithful. Charles Sidney Leary, the minister of public works from 1939 to 1941, unwisely put it in writing, but no one seemed to notice. Both Leary's business and political dealings got him into trouble, but he was a survivor throughout.

Rolf Walgren Bruhn was the only public-works road superintendent to enter politics and become minister of public works (1929-1932 and 1941-1942). It is hard to imagine what the district engineers thought of his appointment. He worked on the roads before and after becoming a politician. He did not survive his last term, dying in office in 1942.

Frank Mitchell MacPherson is the one minister of public works (1933 to 1939) about whom there is very little information. It is thought that he was the brains behind the arrangement whereby travellers to and from the interior of the province were effectively exempted from paying tolls on the Pattullo Bridge. He exerted his influence in the backroom, where a lot of political business was conducted in British Columbia prior to the Second World War.

fiscal year 1933-34 states, a "key man" imported to each project to "control the engineering features" of their work.

When the relief camps settled in from 1933 through 1934, life in them was really not that bad. These single men (and some married ones surreptitiously among them) worked a five-day week, seven hours a day. Sometimes the wives and children of the "unsingle" ones camped out nearby them in the summer; certainly on the Hope-Princeton east end they did, where there were 12 work camps spread out over 25 miles.[5]

The food was adequate, as was the housing and the clothing, and a doctor visited them once a week (and probably the wives and children too), but the monotony and the apparent endlessness of it was mind-boggling. That is why in April of 1935, after a winter of heavy snow, 400 of these men without hope left their work and set out from Princeton, picking up others en route on a peregrination to Vancouver. They walked most of the way, or hitchhiked, or rode the trains illegally. They had to do something. The trigger was the action taken by the Prime Minister of Canada, R.B. Bennett, in 1934 when he put forward legislation defining a voter in a Dominion election as someone domiciled in Canada, and a relief camp did not qualify as a domicile. In other words, he disenfranchised all the men in these camps. This was the last straw.[6]

The Relief Camp Workers Union, led by Arthur Evans, had held a series of strikes over the previous year. In the spring of 1935 Evans launched a relief camp strike across the province. Bands of young men began arriving in Vancouver on April 4, 1935, insisting on a meeting with Prime Minister Bennett to press their demands: the right to vote, improved living conditions, unemployment insurance, and wages of 40 cents an hour. The result was a series of riots in Vancouver. When the mayor of that city, Gerald McGeer, would not arrange food for the strikers, they protested by marching through the streets. They were able to survive on gifts of food and money and moral support from the people of the city. Events came to a head when the strikers occupied the city library on May 18, culminating in what became known as Bloody Sunday. Mayor McGeer finally allowed three days' worth of food relief to be issued, but it was clear that nothing more could be accomplished in Vancouver.

On June 3 about a thousand men swarmed aboard a CPR freight train, filling every box car and crowding the roofs. They set out eastwards to carry their frustration to the nation's capital in the On-to-Ottawa Trek. Most of the men were young, scruffy, and well-experienced at riding freight trains. Their enthusiasm was infectious, and new recruits climbed aboard at every stop as they rolled through the mountains and southern Alberta.

But the R.B. Bennett government and the RCMP regarded with unease these men, who were mostly unmarried, hopeless, and unemployed. Any dissent, no matter how peaceful and justified, was seen as a possible threat to the country. The Bennett government had twice sent the RCMP into Saskatchewan to deal with civil unrest: in Estevan in 1931 and in Saskatoon in 1933 they provoked riots with deadly results as the Mounties used batons, riding crops, and guns to rout protesters.

The On-to-Ottawa Trek was halted in Regina by the RCMP. For two tense weeks the trekkers and the Mounties were caught in a stalemate. A raid on July 1, Dominion Day, saw a peaceful public rally turn into a pitched battle, with the city police firing guns directly into a crowd of rioters. Two people were killed, hundreds more were injured, and thousands of dollars' worth of damage was done to the city.

Nearly two dozen of the trekkers went to trial, but the majority just trickled back to the camps that summer. Work started up again out of Hope and Princeton and elsewhere. The annual reports of the department of public works do not mention the hunger marches, the riots, and the occupation of government premises that took place up to 1935 and after.

The next year, 1936, saw the implementation of the "coastal unemployment" federal relief program, which was designed to help a battered Vancouver City Council deal with the seasonal influx of homeless men from elsewhere in the country who came seeking the warmer weather of the Coast in winter.[7] In 1938, two winters and a spring later, these men, forgotten and ostracized by a society finally emerging from its doldrums, were to bring about the final extravaganza of their frustration incurred by the Great Depression.

Again on a Sunday, and again on a bloody one, June 18, 1938, 800 homeless, destitute, and desperate men who had occupied the Hotel Georgia, the Vancouver Post Office, and the Vancouver Art Gallery in a sit-down strike were forcibly evicted. This horde of shouting and blood-spattered men, running before a barrage of Vancouver Police with their batons and tear-gas bombs, erupted into a frenzy of window-smashing and looting that went on all day. When the day was over, 38 of them were in hospital, 23 were behind bars, and downtown merchants were faced with a damage bill of $50,000, or a million of today's dollars.[8]

Prominent among Pattullo's road problems was the very poor showing on the Hope-Princeton project by the men from the relief camp a few miles east of Hope, one of the most rambunctious camps of them all, and the one most subject to strikes and slowdowns. An ordinance map that appeared in 1939 shows only 6½ miles of acceptable roadway completed out of Hope, compared to 28½ miles of reconstruction (of an existing rough road) from Princeton easterly, but none of it was finally finished. Of the 52 miles left, 42 were a "pioneer road" (today it would be generous to class this as a minimum-standard access road), and the last 10 miles had no road.[9]

Under the bright skies of 1929, Nelson Lougheed, in one of his infrequent pronouncements, had promised the residents along this road that construction would start in 1930 and be completed in two to three years. They never let him forget this when nothing happened that year, or later when the relief crews produced so little, and they eventually carried forward their frustration to Pattullo. They were rather set back by the Depression, but by 1936 they started up again, and they were furious when the whole thing was forgotten when the camps were closed down that year.[10]

By 1938 they had a full-fledged public relations movement underway with meetings, letters to the editor, and full coverage by the media. When the relief camps closed down, the department of public works commented in their annual report for that year: " ... from the point of view of getting results this method is not so satisfactory as the normal way ... " The missing link between Hope and Princeton came to be known as "the great procrastination."

Duff Pattullo showed a high degree of fortitude in starting the building of a high-level road bridge across the Fraser River at New Westminster in 1935, a handsome structure that would eventually be named after him. The estimated cost was $4 million, exactly the same figure as the entire roads budget of the province in 1929, which had been its last prosperous year. The bridge eventually cost $6 million. The financial shock was to be lessened by the collection of tolls, but this relief would come later. If Pattullo thought that the bridge would bring him plaudits, he was mistaken. The good old Vancouver Terminal City Club members were very upset with him for the spin-off of dollars elsewhere, their minds being that much more localized by their economic nervousness. Their feelings were echoed by the Interior communities, and even more forcibly by their desperate unemployed.

The Pattullo Bridge was a necessary luxury, since it replaced a railway bridge with a single-lane roadway subject to a load restriction for trucks. This low-level structure had been built by the Great Northern Railway in 1903, and they had signed up the Canadian Northern (later known as the Canadian National) and the interurban line as equal partners in its use. It was also a swing bridge, subject to frequent openings. It was not surprising that the congestion and delays in the use of it by both road and rail were horrendous. Duff Pattullo should have been acclaimed as a saviour for replacing it, but he was not—the "Dirty Thirties" were like that![11]

When these haunted, unhappy men came to the coast in the hot summer of 1935, they had loudly demanded the resignation of their premier for committing $4 million to a bridge, an amount that they said should have come from Ottawa. They said their government's money would have much better been used to help them province-wide. This criticism was tragically unfair. Throughout the economic emergency, Pattullo had steadfastly urged the national government to commit a total of $200 million to public-works projects throughout the country to offset the distress of these men. His pleas had been ignored, and any assistance to his urgently needed bridge had been refused. But desperate men, without hope and denied work year after year, are not inclined to be fair.

What was especially hurtful to this proud man, always immaculately dressed and turned out, was that this condemnation

### The Pattullo Bridge

This classic drawing of the Pattullo Bridge was taken from the 1935 annual report of the department of public works; it was obviously done before the bridge was named after Premier Pattullo. It is rather poignant that no one really thanked him for it, because it was desperately needed and would become a wonderful asset to the province. The problem was that Depression-struck citizens begrudged the money spent on it, and they thought that the Dominion government should have paid for it. It was estimated at $4 million and cost $6 million. The "Y" intersection at the north end, which caused many accidents, was still there in the 1950s. From its opening in 1937 it was a toll structure, until Premier W.A.C. Bennett removed the tolls.

had come from the loggers, the sawyers, and the cannery workers—possibly the same men, and more like them, who had elected and re-elected him faithfully in Prince Rupert from 1916 onwards. Pattullo was a liberal with a small "l" as well as a capital one, and this shook his confidence to the core; he never really recovered from it.

In effect he was trying to bring a "new deal" to British Columbia in the footsteps of F.D. Roosevelt and economist John Maynard Keynes, who had enlightened the generous thinkers of the world in the '30s by his maxim that public investment stimulated employment. W.A.C. Bennett attested to Pattullo's restraint and resolution in this crisis (and possibly also to a liking for Keynes), when he said that he had always admired Pattullo, and Bennett did not form this opinion readily for those of the Liberal cause.

.NEW WESTMINSTER BRIDGE.1936.

Pattullo made a move at this time that eventually brought about his political demise. He decided to scrape together all the funds that he could find and embark on a program of small public-road improvement projects widely spread throughout the province as his answer to this criticism. After the army left in 1936, the department of public works called a total of 37 contracts throughout the province, all for the reconstruction of existing roads. The total price tag for them came to $1.7 million, which was an indication of how limited in mileage these individual projects had to be. The average was $35,000 per contract (seven under $10,000), and for this amount 138 miles of roadway were reconstructed, an average of less than four miles per job. In this day and age such figures for contracts would be unbelievable.[12]

But to the road foremen, the purveyors of roadwork patronage in those days, and to Frank Mitchell MacPherson, their champion, they were like lifebelts thrown to drowning men. The days of the army running things were over. Patronage in road-building contracts blossomed in British Columbia, and extreme pressure came along with it to hire local Liberal-Party supporters, who felt that they, before anyone else, were entitled to "work and wages"—a Pattullo slogan he would soon regret. Of course many of these contractors were party supporters who were neither sufficiently experienced nor equipped to carry out the work. The 1930s were not good years in which to find road builders who were adequately outfitted and ready to go.

The patronage was widespread in those days, particularly in centres remote from the district headquarters, where it sometimes progressed to misuse of government equipment and materials. One Liberal cabinet minister from the Interior was reported to have regularly used trucks owned by the department of public works to haul produce from his fields to his farm. The district engineers did not have much chance of finding evidence of such misdeeds by unexpectedly arriving at the scene. There was little traffic on the roads, and their use for an unheralded inspection trip did not go undetected, especially when a department ferry was used; the phones would bring a warning. Similar early warnings of headquarters inspectors coming in from Victoria also took place, even if they came in from the United States, because there were also telephones in the customs houses.

These were close-knit communities in the Interior, and there was distrust for anyone coming from Victoria or the Lower Mainland. Of course, the local member of the legislature was often involved. Unfortunately, there was distrust for the district engineer as well, he too being sent by Victoria. This dislike and suspicion of Victoria in the Interior was a consequence of the actions of the Kidd and the Economy committees in the Depression and war years and was a major reason for the success of the Social Credit party.

For this and his contract program, Pattullo got little but disfavour from the public, including many of the Liberal-Party membership throughout the interior of the province. It was one factor in his rejection at the leadership convention in 1941. This political treachery saw him ousted as leader of the party, despite his dedicated service to British Columbians, which won the 1937 election for the Liberals and brought them the most members, but left them four short of a clear majority in 1941. He was also held to blame for a denial of Dominion government money due to his rejection of the Rowell Sirois report, which would have given much more control of provincial funding to the senior government.[13] In all of this he lost the friendship of William Lyon Mackenzie King, one that dated back many years to a family relationship.

Pattullo was convinced that he could engender sufficient support from the newly emerging CCF party to carry on, but his party and especially his former good friend John Hart did not think so, and they turned on him. There was no way that Duff Pattullo was going to ally himself with the Conservatives, with whom he had battled for five years as leader of the Opposition. He resigned as premier and thereafter sat as an independent member in the legislature in Victoria until the election of 1945, wherein he lost his seat. That all of this happened at the same time as Pearl Harbor did not help the situation. John Hart, the minister of finance up until then, became premier on Pattullo's departure.

A cartoon in the Vancouver *Province* October 8, 1941, depicts a paved road section appearing before a motorist who is shown driving on a rough gravel surface. The driver expresses his delight at the approaching pavement, shown by encircled text, "Ah, at last, a place where votes were needed!" Neil McCallum, who became the chief engineer in public works in 1949 after being the paving engineer for the City of Vancouver, said that there were no pavements of any value at all throughout the interior of the province before the Second World War. Another factor against Pattullo was the behaviour of his minister of public works, Charles Sidney Leary, particularly regarding the Big Bend Highway, the opening of which Leary needlessly delayed for patronage purposes.

Pattullo's folly was that he let all of this happen, although there was really nothing else he could have done in positive action. He needed more provincial funding as the solution to his problems, and it was just not there. He should have lessened, if not stopped, the patronage. Once again a premier of the province had gone to the wall over transportation issues. His treatment again demonstrated the cruelty that sometimes comes to those who practice politics in British Columbia. As a final blow, Prime Minister Mackenzie King refused an application from his admirers in the party to have Pattullo appointed to the Senate. This premier did a great deal for his beloved province in very difficult times, and for Canada, but he died some years later a broken man.

As a footnote to this business of some privileged people obtaining work on the roads through politics, a lot can be learned from the book *The Squire of Kootenay West*, by Maurice Hodgson.

The squire in question was H.W. (Bert) Herridge, who had been the vice-president of the Liberal Party in B.C. before he left them, joined the CCF, and became the member for Rossland-Trail riding in the 1941 election. The reason Herridge changed sides during that campaign was patronage, and more particularly that practised by the Liberal member running for re-election in the Kaslo Slocan riding, the aforementioned Charles Sidney Leary, a sawmill owner in the B.C. Interior.

Leary had gotten himself into very hot water for his handling of his bankrupted sawmill in Nakusp, which he tried to have purchased by another mill owned by himself in Revelstoke. Herridge had been part of a group that had thwarted this illegal move, so no love was lost between him and Leary. Herridge confided to author Hodgson that when Leary campaigned in the 1928 election, which he lost, Leary sent out a letter to his faithful supporters stating, in part: " ... [I]f you elect me ... there will be considerably more patronage shown to my boys than during my last term ... " [14] Spurred on by such philosophy among the Liberals, the hiring and firing really started up under the Conservatives when they gained power.

Herridge said that for years he had witnessed the placement and displacement of road gangs, clerks, petty officials, and even administrators in the civil service in the Slocan and Kootenay areas. In the book it becomes evident that one of those fired was Herridge himself. (He was for some time a road foreman.) Leary came to the legislature once more with the Liberals in 1933, stayed in office, and was re-elected in 1941. After MacPherson, Pattullo held the position for a short time, then Leary was appointed minister of public works in 1939, and he stayed in that office until 1941.

In this position, Leary stubbornly delayed the opening of the Big Bend Highway (built by the Canada Parks Branch and presented to the province) in favour of last-minute small contracts. These were being let for very flimsy asphalt surfacings near inhabited areas, which did not last for more than a few months. It can only be surmised that this was a hangover from the surfacing contracts let by Pattullo in 1936.

There was an interesting sidelight to the opening of the King George VI Highway (previously known as the Peace Arch Highway) in October of 1940, when Leary was minister. The lavish banquet put on at that time by the department was recalled many years later by a draftsman in the New Westminster office. He was assigned to attend the banquet as a waiter, decked out in a suitable uniform! In those days the word of the civil servants' masters was law. Of course there was no union, just an employee's association, which was obviously much more submissive.

After the 1941 election, and after the coalition of Liberals and Conservatives came about, a man called Thomas King was minister for a short time. Then Rolf Bruhn got the job for a second time (he was minister from 1929 to 1932 under Tolmie), but he died in August of 1942. John Hart, after doing the job himself for a short while, made the very good move of appointing Herbert Anscomb, the leading Conservative, to the position. Anscomb turned out to be an exceptionally good roads administrator. Hart first of all offered the job to a then-little-known MLA from Kelowna, W.A.C. Bennett, but he refused it because he could not leave his hardware business at that stage of its expansion.

The start of the war in the fall of 1939 was a relief to Pattullo because by then the demand for the Hope-Princeton link had reached its crescendo. All that Pattullo needed to say was that its start would await the end of hostilities. This handy way out of all commitments for roads was a relief to John Hart as well when he took over, because it could be used to stop another nagging want, one not altogether supported by the people to be served by it. This was the building of a highway from the rest of British Columbia to the Peace River Block, a long-term unrealized dream for Pattullo that he handed down to John Hart.

Duff Pattullo had taken part as minister of lands in the rather hilariously reported trip made by Premier Harlan Brewster to the Peace River Block in September of 1917. It was quite an adventure, because to get there without leaving the province, they had to go right back to the travel mode of the first pioneers who passed that way 124 years before, the foremost of whom was of course Alexander Mackenzie. They travelled by canoe from the end of the road near Summit Lake north of Prince George by the Crooked River, the Parsnip River, and the Peace River, with a hike on a trail around the Peace River Canyon portage. At the downstream end of the canyon, at a settlement called Hudson's Hope, they were met by a large and elegant sternwheeler named the *D.A. Thomas* that took them downstream from there. (This vessel had been built by the man of the same name, who later became Lord Rhonda, a coal-mining tycoon from Wales.)[15]

Thomas had spent $250,000 in geologic surveys looking for coal and oil in the region and had just given up and returned to Britain the year before. He had drilled for oil near Fort Vermilion without success, although he had great success in finding coal. His namesake vessel cost him $119,000 to build and gave good service, although it was really too large for any use proposed for it; it was eventually run aground and abandoned in 1930 some years after being purchased by the Hudson's Bay Company.

Pattullo, whose ministry was in charge of oil exploration, was inspired by this experience and what he learned of Thomas's exploits to try his hand. The hole that he had a contractor drill to seek the magical fluid north of Hudson's Hope in 1919 was a dry one.

Greatly discouraged, he did not try again and eventually gave up the dream of finding oil. Many years later Pattullo heard a rumour, which he believed, that somehow the oil industry had infiltrated this attempt by government to get into their business and that the drill site had been deliberately moved about 20 miles away from where it should have been. It was said that this revelation depressed Pattullo greatly in his final years. The oil industry did not find a producing well in the Peace River area until 1951, near Fort St. John. Within 10 years there were over 200 wells in production. In later years Pattullo passed on an interest in the Peace River to his finance minister, who became his successor—an interest that was to bear fruit for the province quite soon.[16]

The Coalition that followed the 1941 election was truly that. The Liberal and Conservative members shared cabinet positions, although the more numerous Liberals retained the premiership. Then in the 1945 and 1949 elections, each party provided Coalition candidates, winning 36 out of 48 seats. The Co-operative Commonwealth Federation (later renamed the New Democratic Party) formed the Opposition in the House, since they refused to join the Coalition;

they won 10 seats in 1945, and the "others" had 2. In the election of 1949 the Opposition lost three seats, the Coalition won three, and the "others" stayed the same. John Hart became the first premier for the Coalition, and Byron Johnson succeeded him in 1947, remaining in office until 1952, when the Coalition finally collapsed.

John Hart, a stockbroker before he went into politics, proved to be an excellent premier. He ran what was described by the leading journalist of the day, Bruce Hutchinson, as the most efficient administration in 25 years. He came to the office of premier in December of 1941 and stayed there until the same month in 1947. He met the problem of hiring road crews, etc., quite simply: the member for each riding controlled that issue among his own people in his own territory. Thereby neither Liberal nor Conservative could accuse the other of preference, and all was quiet. In any event there was little money for them to work with and very few materials or personnel to go with it. Almost all the able-bodied men had gone to the war. As far as road transportation was concerned, Hart surpassed McBride in doing what was needed at the time and nothing more.

Before he resigned in 1947 because of ill health, he had started both the Hart Highway and the link between Hope and Princeton, getting down to work as soon as men, materials, and equipment became available. These two excellent transportation facilities were to contribute more for the province than did any of McBride's railways. The new premier was mindful of the error made by his predecessor,

John Hart, B.C.'s 23rd premier (December 1941 to December 1947) had been a businessman and a finance minister for many years, He also took over public works for a short time (1941 to 1942) while he was premier. The genial Irishman was good at all these tasks. He started the Hart Highway between Prince George and Dawson Creek, the long-awaited link to the Peace River Block. He did not finish it, but it was named after him anyway. A realist, he turned away from Pattullo when coalition was indicated.

Premier Pattullo, who called a great number of very small road contracts, none of which were big enough to attract bids from outside the province. Anxious not to make them too many and too short in mileage, Hart made them too few and too long.

This brought disaster to two successful bidders, one on a 94-mile section and the other on the adjacent 57 miles; the two sections met at the Pine Pass. These were huge lengths of new road construction in difficult, undeveloped, and heavily forested land. Along with lead-up sections reconstructed at either end, they made up an important new route that covered 210 miles.[17]

Even when they participated together in a joint venture, these overextended road builders still went broke. Inadequate access to the start of their work was one of their major problems. They went to litigation, and they were saved from bankruptcy when a judge ruled that the enactment of an Hours of Work statute in B.C., after they had tendered, entitled them to a 30 percent greater payment for what they had finished. Rebid, the contracts were eventually completed. Started in August of 1946, the Hart Highway was not ready for use until July 1952.

In the south the 84 miles from Hope to Princeton was let in two contracts, and as well as this, a 23-mile long contract was put forth from Princeton to Hedley. The Hope-Princeton Highway was started early in 1946 and completed in the fall of 1949. It had no failures of contractors, but it cost about 166 percent more than estimated. The Hart Highway was 150 percent over the estimate. That all of this road construction was carried out to the highest design standards (standards notably missing on the Big Bend Highway) was due largely to Herbert Anscomb, a man who knew his own mind and could see beyond immediate needs. Both premiers in office during this construction, Hart and Johnson, came out smelling like roses in the euphoria of getting good roads—in particular, these two much-needed road connections. They owed this to a man whom neither of them really liked.

In an interesting variation of the trip by Brewster and Pattullo to Hudson's Hope in 1917, Anscomb also visited that pioneer village in 1943, but he went the long way around. Because the United States was then at war, he had to get special permission to drive through

Herbert Anscomb, Premier Byron Johnson, and Ernest Crawford Carson stand at the summit of Allison Pass for the opening of the Hope-Princeton Highway on November 2, 1949. Anscomb was the minister of finance at that time, but had been minister of public works when the highway was started. Carson was the current minister of public works and remained in that position until 1952, the year that P.A. Gaglardi took office.

their territory to Alberta and also to purchase gasoline along the way. He then travelled by the Northern Alberta Railway from Edmonton to Dawson Creek—the only reliable way to go, especially in the spring. Finally he set out by car with a companion driver from Pouce Coupe to Hudson's Hope, only to come to grief in a mudhole several miles short of his destination.

Anscomb and his driver carried on by foot. A few miles along the way they met a young Native girl who had been badly mauled by a grizzly bear. The minister of public works stayed with her and the other man went for help. This was a necessary but courageous action, because the bear could well have returned at any time. On this trip Anscomb represented B.C. at the opening of the bridge built by the Americans over the Peace River at Taylor Flats on the Alaska Highway.[18]

Byron Johnson, also a Liberal, led the Coalition to a victory at the polls in 1947, largely because the economy was recovering so well after the war, and fortunately before the 1948 flood set B.C. back. Johnson was a builder's supply merchant from the Lower Mainland,

As minister of public works (1942 to 1946) throughout the war, Herbert Anscomb had neither the men, materials, nor money to work with, but he still planned well for the future and travelled and met with the public. He was a good minister, but not a comfortable colleague for the Coalition cabinet, nor at times for his fellow Conservatives.

and he turned out to be a good premier, although he was so quiet and self-effacing that people could barely remember his name when he first came into politics. He was of Icelandic origin and his first name was actually Bjorn, changed to Byron by the prejudice of the times. The diminutive of Bjorn was Bjosse in Iceland and this was changed to "Boss"—a nickname that stuck. Unfortunately, many people think to this day that this nickname carries the American political connotation, which in that country means a politician who dominates and manipulates dishonestly. For this man, nothing could be further from the truth.

Johnson set up a post-war rehabilitation council that travelled the province seeking public input. Among its recommendations were a power commission to replace the B.C. Electric Company, which eventually came about and was good for the province, and a recommendation to extend the PGE railway to Alaska, which was not completed; in its final evolution (going only as far as Fort Nelson), it was not an asset. This was an unfortunate premier, not that he died in office, but that he came so close to it. Boss Johnson was in a serious car accident near the end of his term. He survived, but was never the same after it and in his last years suffered from poor health and a lack of funds in his retirement. W.A.C. Bennett most kindly, and with some difficulty, arranged for a pension of $5,000 a year for him in 1959.[19]

Highway building came into its golden age under Johnson. But sad to say, internal conflict within the Coalition, mostly centred around Anscomb, along with public fury at the introduction of a retail sales tax and contributory premiums to a health-insurance

Premier Byron Ingemar Johnson, B.C.'s 24th premier (December 1947 to August 1952), was a modest, well-meaning man, and fully effective as a premier. If John Hart had the Hart Highway named after him, Johnson had a good claim to have the Hope-Princeton be his avenue to immortality. But Johnson Highway would have been just as poor a name for the Hope-Princeton as Prince George-Dawson Creek would have been for the Hart Highway. It's all in how it rolls off the tongue.

system, led to the ousting of the Coalition in 1952. This opened the door for William Andrew Cecil Bennett, who would be the greatest road builder of them all.

Bennett obviously had sympathy for Liberal Byron Johnson but as it turned out, he scarcely had that for his fellow Conservative, Herbert Anscomb. After Rolf Bruhn died, Bennett's man for public works had been Ernest Carson, a fellow-Interior member from Lillooet, and he had been disappointed when Anscomb got the job. Nevertheless, he should have been grateful to the man from Victoria for his high standards and for authorizing the survey to extend the highway along the international boundary after completing it to Princeton. Anscomb followed through later with funding for this extension when he was minister of finance.

Herbert Anscomb was the mayor of Victoria from 1928 to 1931; his family had come to B.C. from the north of England. He was a man who did a great deal for the province but got very little thanks for it. However, his efforts permitted the Reverend Phil Gaglardi, Bennett's Heaven-sent road builder, to get off on the right foot.

Nonetheless, it should not be forgotten that it was what George Woodcock described in *British Columbia: A History of the Province* as "the most efficient administration for twenty-five years" (John Hart's, from 1941 to 1947) and the good efforts of the rather unfortunate Bjosse Johnson for five years after that, that really paved the way for British Columbia's golden years under W.A.C. Bennett.

## Detail of Unemployment Relief Roadwork, 1930 to 1936

### 1930

Relief work began in B.C. when 15,300 men were engaged throughout the province to do general roadwork. The Dominion provided $1 million for this, to be split between the province and the municipalities. The province set up an amount of $500,000 for the department of public works and a similar amount to the municipalities, who themselves contributed $1.2 million.

### 1931

The number of men employed rose to 21,000. Initially they were paid $2 per day with an extra 80 cents if they had dependents. On November 1 this program was shut down because the cost of it had ballooned. The unemployed were moved into relief camps and each man was paid $7.50 per month with free board and lodging, clothing, and medical attention. The funding for this was as follows: Dominion government, $3 million; provincial government, $2.2 million; municipal government, $800,000. The actual expenditure for this year was reported as $2.2 million for 8 million man-hours of work (27.5 cents per man-hour).

### 1932

The unemployed relief work on provincial roads in this year was primarily from the relief camps. The largest of these were at either end of the Hope-Princeton highway link that was under construction, and at the west end of the Big Bend highway at Revelstoke, which was also being built then. That project was split in half at the small settlement called Boat Encampment; the western half of the work from Revelstoke to that point was for the province to build and the eastern half to Golden, for the Canada Parks Branch to build. These were the major relief projects, although there were others.

### 1933

On June 1 the province handed over control for all work from the camps to the Canadian Department of National Defence. The province kept the ownership of its road equipment and responsibility for its maintenance. The department of public works placed key personnel on the projects "to control the engineering features" (Report of the Chief Engineer in the Report to the Minister of Public Works, Fiscal Year 1933-34). In September there were 4,147 men working out of the camps and in January, 1934, 7,783 men. On the Hope-Princeton western end, the section from Mile 4 to Mile 10 was finished—the work was described as "sketchy." At the Princeton end, a length of 29 miles was partially completed and what was called a "pioneer road" was built beyond it. The highway link was a total of 87 miles long, with Allison Pass located close to Mile 40. The provincial government contributed $1 million to this year's work throughout the province.

**1934**

Work from the relief camps continued. There was exceptionally heavy snowfall in the lower Fraser Valley and this led to serious flooding when it melted; Chilliwack was completely cut off for one month. Twenty-four miles of main road were built and 123 miles were improved. The maximum number of men in the camps at one time was 7,142. The province contributed $1 million towards relief roadwork this year.

**1935**

The Dominion government took over all of the Big Bend highway work on the western sector, except for the design and construction of the bridges. The work eastwards out of Hope was completed to Mile 10. There were more bad storms and flooding affecting Kamloops, the north Okanagan, and the Skeena districts. The highest population in the camps was 6,005. The province put up $1.3 million towards the cost of relief work this year.

**1936**

The department of national defence closed down all the relief camps. The payout this year was $2.15 million, $1.15 million by the Dominion government. A special $466,000-program of roadwork on relief from camps in the coastal areas of B.C. was initiated, and run by the province. The men were paid $2.40 for an eight-hour day, less 75 cents for board. Payroll held back $4 per week of this for a certain period (adjusted to the number of dependents) until they considered the man had built up a sufficient holdback to see him through the winter and then he was let go. Work was done on the Lougheed Highway, the West Coast road on Vancouver Island, the Jones Hill revision on the Trans-Canada Highway near Hope, the Spences Bridge-to-Merritt road, the Lytton-to-Lillooet road, the Sechelt-to-Pender Harbour road, and the Squamish-to-Britannia road. A pilot road to Allison Pass from the western end of the Hope-Princeton link was also opened up this year. In addition to this activity, unemployed men were put to work on the Kingsgate-to-Radium road in the East Kootenays, part of a federal/provincial tourist road program to which the Dominion government contributed $200,000. This program encouraged Americans to drive up from the United States, and a popular destination for honeymooning couples was the Banff Springs Hotel—hence the improved road from Kingsgate to Banff National Park.

Note: Most of the above is taken from the annual reports of the department of public works for the fiscal years 1930-31 through 1936-37.

## Chapter Four

# The Bond Burner and the Dreamer: 1952 to 1975

*"True direct democracy is that the elected must govern, and must not be governed by the electors."*
—Premier W.A.C. Bennett

*"I'm learning. I'm learning."*
—Premier Dave Barrett, when asked how he would handle the position of finance minister as well as that of premier

When William Andrew Cecil Bennett became premier in 1952, his Social Credit party had 19 seats to the CCF's 18; 10 were shared among the Liberals and Conservatives. A deciding re-election followed in 1953, and Social Credit triumphed, winning 28 seats to the CCF's 14; the others were reduced to 6. Bennett announced that his major priorities were to ensure B.C. had sufficient electric power available to all of its citizens at reasonable cost and that all means of transportation in the province would be immediately improved, particularly highways.

The first Premier Bennett, William Andrew Cecil (August 1952 to August 1972), brought steady progress to the economic front as well as to the waters of Georgia Strait. B.C.'s 25th premier's finest achievement in transportation was first known as the B.C. Ferries Division of the Department of Highways and later became the B.C. Ferry Corporation. He also brought in the golden age of highway and bridge construction in B.C.

In his anxiety about the public's feelings about road contracts, first from Pattullo's misadventures before the war and second from the Hart Highway and the Hope-Princeton problems after it, Premier Bennett took some very early action on highway contracts. He fully involved his brand-new highways minister, the Reverend Philip Arthur Gaglardi, the new MLA for Kamloops.

That Gaglardi would introduce himself into and last so long in what had been a rather placid pool of politics in Kamloops ruled over by the Fulton family, was a good example of personality over tradition. A Pentecostal minister, Gaglardi's daily religious hour on afternoon radio turned out to be the best hour of their day for a huge number of Kamloops housewives. His popularity soared, and he promptly turned this public support to his political benefit.

That he easily demolished E. Davie Fulton's support provincially 10 years later was a measure of his continuing popularity. Fulton's

The Reverend Phillip Arthur Gaglardi, minister of highways from 1952 to 1968, oversaw and was fully involved in the supervision of road contracts, but the last word on expenditures was always that of Premier Bennett—until it was that of the provincial judge who reprimanded the minister, who had authorized a payment to a contractor after the court had ruled that no more payments should be made. This type of incident finally estranged Bennett from his minister of highways.

father, grandfather, and great-uncle had all been cabinet ministers in Canadian federal politics. Fulton's demise in provincial politics was pursued enthusiastically by both Gaglardi and Bennett in 1963. Fulton, a true blue Conservative, was anxious to banish this upstart, right-wing Social Credit contender for his area. Gaglardi of course was helped by being the pastor of the largest Calvary Temple in the West, although one hitch was that he was a converted Catholic, while Fulton was a more steadfast type. Fulton turned from federal politics to the provincial field in 1963, and not only did he take on Gaglardi in Kamloops, he similarly challenged Bennett province-wide. He failed on both fronts.[1]

Gaglardi quickly became aware of the nuances of road-contract bidding and management but surprisingly, his leader, Premier Bennett, never seemed to get the hang of it. Bennett demonstrated this very early on when he made public the unit prices bid on a winning tender awarded by Social Credit and compared them to those of a contract let by the previous, Coalition government for work in the same area. (Unit prices are the charges listed by the contractor for the various items, such as the cost of a ton of gravel, etc. Normally only the total bid for all items is released.)

He said his government had obtained better prices than his corrupt predecessors. Whether they did or not, and the reason for it could be one of many, unit prices are traditionally kept confidential in road-contract management. Successful contractors do not like

### Those Wacky Three Lanes

Premier W.A.C. Bennett was without doubt the only first minister ever to build a three-lane highway in British Columbia with nary a hill on it. He insisted that the improved roadway planned to serve Victoria from the new ferry terminal at Swartz Bay at the north end of the Saanich peninsula have three lanes, instead of the four recommended by the engineers.

When asked why, he responded that only one lane was needed to drive out to the ferry, but when that ferry unloads all those cars at the same time, two lanes were needed to drive away from it. There was no doubt some logic to this, although not much, but the man at the top was adamant, so the 15 miles of road were built with one lane northbound and two lanes southbound.

Some months later, however, when the premier's attention was firmly engaged elsewhere, the engineers quietly added a lane, at considerable additional trouble and expense, and the Pat Bay Highway had four lanes. It will very likely soon have six.

This was only one of the many "problems with premiers" that plagued the building of the B.C.'s transportation system; sadly, many of the others were more difficult to fix.

them made public, mostly because this knowledge often ends up helping future competitors in subsequent contract calls.[2]

In another way, Bennett was equally obtuse: he would never agree to bonuses for quick work, even when such perks would have led to savings.

When bids are reviewed prior to an award being made and are unexpectedly high or low, several things are considered. The bidder may simply have made a mistake and, when apprised of this, may withdraw his bid, although there are penalties for that. Alternatively, the practice of unbalanced bidding might be detected. This happens when the contractor's estimator believes that the government engineers have miscalculated something, for example the amounts of solid rock and other materials required. An astute bidder can make a lot of money if he surmises this and the extent of it correctly.

If, for example, he believes twice as much solid rock is required (and consequently less of other materials) than has been estimated by the government, he will bid high on rock and low on the other. If he is correct, he will get a bonus on the extra rock paid for and lose less on the amount of other materials excavated, thereby profiting by the contracting process as well as by being the low bidder. The loser in all of this is often the government, which incurs an overrun on that job. Some authorities reject bids for unbalanced bidding, which is often a device leading to claims for additional payments later.

Bennett was the finance minister for almost all of his term and was therefore the final authority on bid acceptance. He steadfastly refused to accept anything other than the lowest bid, and if there was any doubt at all, he insisted that all bids be thrown out and the job rebid. Awkward as this was, it successfully got rid of unbalanced bidding and some other subtleties of contract-winning practice. This practice resulted in the contracting of roadwork for the golden years of road building in British Columbia, the Bennett years, the cleanest on record. Later on, however, towards the end of his reign, Bennett set up a special task force of Treasury Board staff to monitor Gaglardi's road contracts.

A popular saying in those days was that these roads came by the grace of "Ginter, Gaglardi and God," and the reader is left to ponder the meaning of this. Ben Ginter was a road contractor from Prince George who not only won contracts for roads, but also rented out much of his equipment for roadwork done by the local highways district engineers or superintendents, who hired that equipment and used their own as well to build roads by a process known as "day labour" (hiring machines by the hour). This practice was particularly evident in the Kamloops district, which was well financed for it. By this, and also by tendering well on many contracts, Ginter prospered, and many said that he broke up a cosy fraternity of road contractors in the province. Amidst all of this, it was a good thing that W.A.C. Bennett, as premier and finance minister combined, was the best guardian of the provincial purse in highway building, and everything else, that British Columbia ever had.[3]

But this is not the whole story; a look at the turbulent days when Gaglardi first became the head of a public works department sheds more light on it. Up until then the department had never experienced a minister who not only was a man of God, but also sincerely believed himself to be the deity in his new office. The first confrontation of the old versus the new involved the highway board. This group of civil servants at the top of the department hierarchy ruled on such matters as pre-qualification of road contractors, classification questions, and the settlement of any claims these contractors may have submitted for extra payments.

In a sincere effort to avoid hiring unqualified entrepreneurs who may have been politically inspired but were without experience or equipment from obtaining road contracts, as had happened under Pattullo, the Coalition government of the '40s had introduced a process of pre-qualification. Contracts were not advertised; instead, a request for bids went out to a special list of contractors.

Getting on this list required that the highway board, chaired by the chief engineer, examine the applicant's experience, resources of personnel and equipment, and financial backing. This was conscientiously done, but of course it quite often brought controversy, since contractors who did not make this preferred status always questioned the reasons.

The first mention of the highway board appears in the department of public works' annual report for 1943, when the Coalition government was in power with Herbert Anscomb as minister. The board was created by statute, and by that legislation, the chief engineer was appointed chairman and received extra remuneration for that duty. It is believed that this legislation was the product of the coalition of political parties. The intention was to place a servant of the legislature in charge of awarding road contracts rather than a minister—possibly a throwback to the abortive attempt in 1924 to have the legislature award road contracts, as described in chapter two.

One member of the legislature who had received several complaints about pre-qualification from the non-qualifiers was the new premier. At the start of his term, on the very first day, he spoke vehemently against patronage in public works, which he unfairly attributed to the top level of the civil service in that department. Not only would he ban secret orders-in-council, he would also abolish pre-qualification of road contractors, a move meant to discredit the highway board. This he did.[4]

Bennett also repealed the legislation that created the highway board and its chairmanship by the chief engineer (and his remuneration for it). Thereafter it was simply a committee of the department that was chaired by the deputy minister. The new chairmanship was at

Gaglardi's specific instruction, one reason for Chief Engineer Neil McCallum's departure. Many in the industry believed that the repeal of this legislation opened the management of road contracts to political manipulation, but no concrete evidence of this ever appeared during Gaglardi's term in office. Rumours of it arose later on, resulting in a legislative committee's investigation that cleared the minister. When his troubles with his highway builder mounted up at that time, it could be said that Bennett was thus the architect of his own misfortunes.[5]

The truth was that pre-qualification of contractors and the practice of letting only a qualified group bid on public highway contracts was a very dangerous political scenario indeed. In those days it was probably only workable in a special situation such as the coalition of political parties in wartime. What Bennett should have done was to abolish pre-qualification and keep the special status of the highway board and its chairman under his scrutiny in order to restrain the free-enterprising enthusiasm of his minister.

In the end, Gaglardi hastened his own departure by permitting a government plane to carry his daughter-in-law while the plane was being flown to the southern United States for a service check. Bennett chose this error in judgement as the vehicle for Gaglardi's transfer from the highways portfolio to minister without portfolio and eventually to welfare minister.

At about this time Gaglardi brought more disfavour upon himself in his riding by using departmental resources for his private properties near Kamloops. He also got into trouble elsewhere in the Interior when it became known that one of his son's motels had been granted a highway access contrary to policy and, furthermore, that Gaglardi's department had produced signs for these motels. All of these misdemeanours came from a belief that he could do no wrong, a mental aberration that stemmed from his ascendancy in the party as a contender for the leadership. Meanwhile the grand old man at the helm aged rapidly from such antics.[6]

In areas of transportation where his highways minister did not distract him, Bennett did much better. When the privately owned ferry service between the mainland and Vancouver Island was brought to a halt by a strike in 1958, he moved against it. He invoked the Civil Defence Act to put the ferrymen back to work.

After this rather drastic legislative action he placed orders with local shipyards for several new ferries, and at the same time he purchased the American-owned Black Ball ferry service between Nanaimo and Horseshoe Bay in West Vancouver.

Thus he created a government-owned operation that launched new vessels in 1960. This eventually became the B.C. Ferry Corporation in 1977, one of the leading ferry services in the world. In 1988 Bennett's creation operated 38 vessels on 26 routes. Although a free-enterpriser at heart, Bennett showed by this action that he was smart enough to realize that if a company is given a monopoly, someone pays, and it is almost always the user. If it is a public service, the public pays, and a smart politician will not have that. It is to B.C.'s loss that some of the premiers following in his wake have not learned that all monopolies in essential public services have to be publicly owned.

Bennett's takeover of the ferries shows that he was what could be called a state capitalist. This is someone who runs a government for the benefit of capitalism, but in his case, to British Columbia's salvation, it was the lesser entrepreneurs, the small-business community, that he favoured. This was easy to understand because he had belonged to this group in private life with his hardware business. Bennett carried no torch for the large corporations, nor did he have much time for the Vancouver business community. In fact he railed against both of them on occasion.

It was very fortunate for the province that this leader, with this philosophy, was in charge throughout the '50s and '60s, because these were decades of economic growth, and his approach to government was peculiarly suitable to the times. It was also fortunate for him to even get elected in 1952 under a banner that was neither Liberal nor Conservative. This was only possible because the population of this western province was not closely tied to either of the old-line parties, as it had grown rapidly since the '30s with a great inflow from outside of Canada. These parties were at that time distracted by the advent of the Co-operative Commonwealth Federation, later to become the New Democratic Party. They felt the socialist hordes were at their doorstep.

Bennett's goal was progressive economic development for the entire province, which he saw as the best way to help small business.

To achieve this he cared not that he was at times labelled a socialist or a dictator. It was towards this end that he nationalized the ferry service to Vancouver Island and took over the B.C. Electric Company, the latter to ensure the extension of rural electrification, and it was for this reason that he put in motion his huge highway program. His feeling was that government enterprise was a means to an end.

He gained the "dictator" label from one pronouncement that he made, as reported in Paddy Sherman's *Bennett*: "True direct democracy is that the elected must govern and must not be governed by the electors ... if the electors govern you have anarchy." Bennett would no doubt have heartily agreed with another quote from an economist: "The small entrepreneur governs private and public bureaucracies."

For the construction of a major highway route south of Vancouver that would contribute to his goal of a fully effective vehicular ferry service to Vancouver Island, Bennett benefited greatly from the vision of one man—not Gaglardi, who claimed it, but from the Social Credit MLA for Delta at that time, an independent spirit by the name of George Massey. Another of Bennett's backbenchers, Cyril Shelford, the member for Omineca (Burns Lake), describes in his book *From Snowshoes to Politics* how Massey collected information from around the world on the subject of tunnels under rivers. Massey was convinced that one could be built under the Fraser River where its channel is divided by Deas Island, alongside his home at Ladner, a small town in his riding near the confluence of the Fraser and the Strait of Georgia. The mayor and council of Ladner were his only supporters; his colleagues in the legislature derided his idea when he first spoke of it.[7]

The tunnel proposal proved to be eminently feasible when a Dutch company stepped forward with a proven and patented method of placing the six huge concrete tunnel sections on a soft sand river bottom such as at Ladner. Gaglardi immediately adopted the idea as his own and strode forward with it. In so doing, he parted company with his chief engineer of public works, who favoured a bridge over the Fraser some miles upstream of Ladner, near to where the Alex Fraser Bridge stands today. When the tunnel went into service, Gaglardi trumpeted that it was a triumph of vision over cold engineering fact, and unfortunately for the engineers supporting Chief Engineer Neil McCallum, it was indeed.[8]

The years from 1957 through the 1960s were the most productive for highways and bridges that British Columbians have ever lived through. Roads were being built to new, higher standards of width, grade, and alignment and they were suitable for speeds of up to 70 miles per hour. One summer there were a total of 62 steel or concrete bridges under contract throughout the province, and few of them were small; British Columbians have many wide rivers to cross. In 1951 there were 30 small ferries crossing rivers in the Interior, all powered by the river current; by 1973 these were down to 9. Almost all of those that disappeared were replaced by bridges—a great tribute to W.A.C. Bennett's overall road program.

Under the financing of the Toll Highways and Bridge Authority (which Bennett created in 1953), the department of highways completed a number of major structures within these years. Numbered among these were the Nelson Bridge, the Agassiz-Rosedale Bridge, the Kelowna Floating Bridge, the Second Narrows Bridge over Burrard Inlet (that structure had problems), as well as the Deas Island Tunnel under the Fraser River. The department also completed the Tsawwassen and Swartz Bay terminals for Bennett's new ferry service and contracted out the building of first two ferries, the *Queen of Tsawwassen* and the *Queen of Sidney*. These ferries were vessels with a capacity of 138 cars and a service speed of 18 knots. One was built in Victoria and the other in Vancouver.[9]

W.A.C. Bennett performed brilliantly in the dual role of premier and finance minister throughout all of this, although most of the credit and all of the glory was taken by his highways minister, Phil Gaglardi. Nonetheless, Flyin' Phil's wings were clipped from time to time. On one occasion when there was a $9 million overrun on the Deas Island tunnel project, incurred with Gaglardi's approval but without reference to Bennett, the premier became furious. He recovered the overrun from the budgets of all the highways districts throughout the province, divided proportionately, except for Gaglardi's Kamloops district, which donated twice as much as the others.

It was unfortunate that Bennett did not rein in Gaglardi more often during the 1960s, since Gaglardi's mission was not just the advancement of the province: his goal was the throne itself.[10] Bennett's control over him lessened as Gaglardi's popularity increased, an increase that was largely due to Bennett's achievements. Bennett lost more and more authority over Gaglardi, mostly because of his practice of delegating power to his ministers in everything but finances.

This was demonstrated early in the decade when the premier summoned to his office the regional highway engineer for the northern half of the province, when that official was visiting Victoria. There, with the personal amiability for which he was noted, he suggested that the highway from Terrace to Hazelton, which was about to be upgraded, be brought to a lesser standard than the rest of the route in order to save money. He asked how much the construction at the lower standard would cost for the 83-mile section. ("Cece" Bennett was so genial that all notions of holding back on him would disappear.) He was given a figure of $10 million, and when funds in that amount were subsequently provided to the ministry, Gaglardi used it as he had always intended, that is, to the full standard.

The ministry's annual reports from 1962 through 1967 show that there were six major grading contracts let on the Terrace-Hazelton section in these years. These resulted in the completion of 40 miles out of the 83.[11] Paving contracts were also let as the grading progressed, as well as contracts for bridges and overpasses. Actual costs are impossible to calculate at this late date, but a conservative estimate of the per-mile cost of grading and paving to the high two-lane standard used in that area then was $300,000 per mile. This would result in a total of $12 million for the 40 miles, with $2 million or $3 million added for bridges and overpasses. Towards Premier Bennett's wish for 83 miles, for which he provided $10 million, they achieved less than half that distance for $15 million.

It is not known whether the premier took his minister to task for this, but if Bennett anticipated having the whole section paved in time for the 1969 election, he was out of luck. Still, Gaglardi built a highway capable of supporting speeds up to 70 miles per hour, whereas the one Bennett wanted was only good for 40 to 50. Why Bennett did not consult with his highways minister initially was not explained. Gaglardi heard of his wishes but was quite unconcerned. The fact that Bennett's dictate was ignored brought no official response from the premier's office. To at least one observer, Gaglardi was ignoring his premier with his eye on the top job even as early as 1964. In this case, his decision, opposed to that of his premier, met with the approval of staff.

It was in the matter of railways that Cece Bennett committed his greatest errors in the realm of transportation. Once more the problem of the Pacific Great Eastern had been handed over to a succeeding premier. John Hart had established from his post-war rehabilitation committee's tour of the province that the people favoured an extension of the PGE to Prince George. This was completed in September of 1952. Bennett immediately started work on an extension north from that centre, which finished up with lines to both Fort St. John and to Dawson Creek, changing the name to the British Columbia Railway in the process. In 1958 Bennett arrived in the Peace River area like a conquering hero—appropriately riding in a presidential railcar, borrowed from an American railway—to drive two last spikes.[12]

It seemed that this experience went to his head, as his desire for more trips in presidential grandeur appeared to surpass his normal good sense. He immediately started planning a rail line north to Fort Nelson, which was marginally economically justifiable, and one west to a dot on the map with the name Dease Lake beside it, which was not. If ever there was a rail line that started nowhere and ended nowhere with nothing in between, it was the proposed line from Summit Lake to Dease Lake. Never finished, it ended up halfway to its destination, and then the project collapsed in a flurry of lawsuits. The elder Bennett was gone before that worked itself out, and his son was fated to convene the necessary court of inquiry, an action he took with great reluctance. Justice Lloyd McKenzie also looked at the line to Fort Nelson, which in many ways was a similar disaster, but one that survived. His conclusions were not complimentary.[13]

Despite these setbacks, Cece Bennett will always be regarded by many British Columbians as the finest premier the province has seen to this date. Despite Gaglardi's excesses, his own approaching old age, and the emerging railway problems in the wilderness, he nonetheless won an election handily in 1969, gaining 38 seats to the New Democrats' 12, 5 more than he had amassed in 1966. In the end, as his biographer David J. Mitchell says, he was misunderstood by a changing society in 1972, the year that he witnessed his party's defeat in tears but retained his own seat. His bluster and gimmickry (who could forget the bond burning on Okanagan Lake in the summer of 1959?) rather sadly concealed a sincere and honest man who worshipped financial probity and hard work, and loved his province. He was replaced by a younger man who could speak well and do little else: Dave Barrett, a former social worker known as "Wee Davey." The difference was dramatic—in style, substance, and longevity.

The bond burning underlines another facet of Bennett's nature: He loved a photo opportunity, and he liked to put on a show with it. Two things came about in 1959 that gave him an opportunity to do this: first, his decision that summer to call an election the next year, and second, a statement jointly made by the deputy minister of finance and the comptroller general of the province. They declared that the public debt of the province was fully provided for by sinking funds that ensured the full payment of all principal and interest— in other words, that the direct legal debt of British Columbia was officially dissolved. Bennett decided to stage a celebration of this, and he did it at Kelowna.

The day he chose was August 1, 1959, a lucky seven years to the day from his assumption of power, and the occasion was Kelowna's great day of the year, the Kelowna Regatta. About $70 million worth of cancelled bonds were brought from the coast by armoured truck (!) and placed on the deck of a small barge, making quite a stack of paper. As dusk fell, a launch carrying Bennett and a cohort of cabinet ministers approached the barge, which was anchored a safe distance from the city's foreshore. The bonds had been carefully soaked in gasoline and were held down by chicken wire. The huge crowd onshore held their breath, as a bow and a flaming arrow were placed in the premier's hands. Unfortunately he could not get the bow to work, so they came closer and he threw the flaming arrow at the bonds. This also did not work, and an RCMP constable who was out of the view of the public surreptitiously put a torch to them. The show went on.

It was a great spectacle and the most memorable of many stunts masterminded by the garrulous publicist William Clancey, who has been described as Social Credit's "court jester." But as the deputy minister of finance and the comptroller general watched on TV, they perhaps pondered the fact that although British Columbia was free of direct debt, the province's guaranteed debt had grown to several hundred million dollars under Bennett. On a per-capita basis, it represented a larger debt than any other Canadian province.[14] But Bennett's economic diligence was paying off, and revenues were blossoming.

A story from Hudson's Hope underlines that although Bennett might have acted like a buffoon at times, he was neither a pompous nor a thoughtless one. On one of his triumphant Peace River trips, he visited the site of the proposed dam in that area, and he decided to drive from Chetwynd, where he had arrived by train. His entourage of three limousines, with his at the head, swept up to the landing of the primitive reaction ferry (soon to be replaced by a bridge) across the Peace River at Hudson's Hope.

When the ferry arrived, Bennett's chauffeur started ahead but the ferryman held up his hand and beckoned forward a very dilapidated automobile carrying several members of the area's Native population—they were there first. Bennett's driver complained loudly, but the premier quickly silenced him. When they were all aboard the ferry, Bennett called the First Nations people over to his car's window and chatted to them in a most friendly fashion all the way across. It was sad indeed that he could not maintain such a casual accord with all British Columbians for all of his time with them, but in his later years their ways of life outpaced him, and he simply lost touch. He was also growing weary.

In accordance with his custom, Bennett went to the voters three years after the time before, and the election, which would be his last, took place on August 30, 1972. The result was shocking: 38 seats for the New Democratic Party (NDP), exactly the number that Social Credit got in 1969. Bennett's total was 10 seats, with 5 seats going to the Liberals and 2 to the Conservatives. It might be said of that election that the New Democrats did not win it: The Social Credit party lost it.[15]

Controversy arose over comments made by Gaglardi, Bennett's foremost burr under the saddle by that time. These were critical of cabinet colleagues and were combined with forecasts of Bennett's early retirement if he won the election. All of these detracted from a team approach and that did not help; nor did Bennett's isolation as he toured the province in lonely magnificence in that limousine with that driver, unaccompanied by other cabinet ministers, an old man by himself. After his tears on election night, he pulled himself together quickly, comforted his staff most graciously, and contemplated retirement. He still retained his Okanagan seat, but not for long. He was the official leader of the Opposition in the new NDP legislature for only 10 months. Twenty years was long enough for any premier—it was time for him to go and he knew it.

Dave Barrett, the first premier from the New Democratic Party in the history of British Columbia, spent only about 1,200 days in power, and he outlined what would be his major transportation-related error right at the start of his term. He announced that his was not going to be a blacktop government; in other words, any priority that the highway system might have enjoyed up to that time was set aside. Dave's priorities, as might be expected, were to be in the area of social services, which for him included union matters, and especially, as might also be expected, those concerning the public-service unions. In this he was greatly assisted by Bob Williams, his friend and supporter who became his minister of lands, forests and water resources, and also of recreation and conservation.

Barrett's government in fact quite soon became known as "Williams, Barrett & Co.," much to the annoyance of the last mentioned. Bob Williams had been a candidate in the very acrimonious leadership contest the NDP had held in 1969 when Robert Strachan, the outgoing

Dave Barrett, the 26th premier (September 1972 to December 1975) did not show any interest in highways, and his feelings about ferries never seemed to rise above his concerns about the welfare of the crews.

party president, was replaced. In this competition, it was the lack of support from Strachan that drew enough votes from Barrett to let Tom Berger emerge victorious, a shock to Barrett. The poor showing of Berger in the election immediately following led to Barrett's emergence as NDP leader before the election of 1972.

Williams was a graduate of the University of British Columbia and had been the town planner for Delta, the municipality spread across the delta of the Fraser River a few miles south of Vancouver. He had also been a councillor of the city of Vancouver and a private planning consultant at the same time. Much more subtle in the pulling of the levers of power than the premier, Williams preferred the wings rather than centre stage. He helped his rather stumbling commander-in-chief arrive at the best possible cabinet choices from the group of New Democrats elected, the majority of whom were from Vancouver or Lower Mainland ridings.

Bob Williams was minister of lands, forests, and water resources, as well as minister of recreation and conservation in the first NDP government (1972 to 1975). He was not a team player, preferring to mastermind Barrett in the background. He conducted a vendetta against the highways department during his short time in office.

When Barrett and Williams reviewed the elected members for appointees to cabinet, it seemed that they were hesitant to fill the numerous portfolios without doubling up even more than Bennett. In fact, they found only 15 to be suitable, including themselves, to replace the 16 that Bennett's cabinet had grown to in 1972. Six of them had double portfolios.[16]

One of his most notable cabinet choices was the former party leader. Robert Strachan, a carpenter foreman from the Nanaimo area on Vancouver Island, became the highways minister, and in addition he acquired the responsibility for transportation, which included B.C. Ferries, then a division of the highways department (which the NDP promptly converted into a Crown corporation). Strachan also acquired the very onerous task of creating and operating the public automobile-insurance service that had been one of the NDP's election promises.

The health of this very fine man suffered under this burden to the extent that he was transferred from highways before a year was out. That he had been so overloaded was just one indication of the adversity that Barrett displayed lengthily to those of his own party who fell out of favour with him. Barrett of course resented Strachan's failure to support him in his leadership bid. For a former party leader the post of finance minister would have been expected, but Barrett retained that portfolio for himself.

Robert Strachan, minister of highways from 1972 to 1975, was a member from Vancouver Island, and his concern during his short stay in charge of the B.C. Ferries division of the department of highways was to hold off a strike. He was removed from that responsibility once he had solved its strike problem and before he had time to do anything else .

The highways department was fortunate to get Strachan at the beginning of the NDP rule, since it was due to him that they initially retained H.T. Miard, their much-respected deputy minister. Bob Strachan appreciated Tom Miard for the fine civil servant that he was, but as soon as Strachan left, Williams added Miard to the 17 other civil service deputy ministers that the NDP government demoted or discharged in the first 12 months in office. Rather than take advantage of this experienced management talent, who were for the most part very anxious to help the new government, the new government threw them out and replaced them with a hodgepodge of appointments drawn from outside of the service.[17]

Among these was one of the consulting fraternity, an engineer who replaced Miard. He came in along with several of Williams's former planning colleagues. There was no need for the NDP to follow the old pre-war parties' precedent of replacing road foremen. The present road foremen were good members of the B.C. Government Employees Union and therefore untouchable, but the NDP had the whole management structure above them to play with!

Few governments in the history of British Columbia have shown the NDP's talent for flooding the civil service with party supporters, and this practice spread to the Crown corporations' management in 1972. It was a recipe for disaster that came to a boil in 1,200 days, when the New Democrats became history at the hands of an outraged electorate incensed by the bungling of many of these political appointees, especially those at the senior level.

There was one more action of little wisdom that Williams and Barrett took. This was the creation of the new position of deputy minister to the premier, a sort of super-civil servant. This innovation had long-lasting effects, as Barrett's successors enthusiastically sustained it. The harm lay in the new system that emerged from it, whereby political deputy ministers were encouraged to bypass their ministers and report to the super deputy, who also controlled all the cabinet committees. This practice diverted less power in the first NDP government because of Williams' dominance, but that changed in the governments to follow. Sadly, most of these super-deputies were recruited from outside of the province.

That British Columbia, with a population equal to New Zealand, should proclaim to all and sundry that it did not have among its own people the ability to run itself was a fallacy, but one that was nevertheless supported by this practice of its premiers from 1972 onwards. Cyril Shelford had experience of this when Bill Bennett extended the practice. In his book he described its effect, which included the weakening of the caucus and backbenchers becoming nothing more than ombudsmen for their ridings.[18]

The one thing that these newcomers to B.C. had in common was their complete lack of knowledge about the province. Their strength was in short-term political decisions. In long-term policy making, requiring a deep familiarity with the province, its people, terrain, and history, their input was minimal and often ill-advised. The effects of this are evident in an ongoing recurrence of disasters of management and policy by the premiers who succeeded Wacky Bennett. It became much less likely that locally insightful and inspired backbenchers such as George Massey would be able to come forward and save the day.

Barrett soon found out that his plan to head a non-blacktop government was one that came much before its time—if there ever was a time for it! The people of the interior of the province still wanted their roads paved, and they made this very clear. The result was a sudden panic to produce paving contracts in the last summer that the NDP was in power, quite similar to Pattullo's commotion of 35 years earlier. No new paving contracts were let in 1974, but contracts for 240 miles of road surfacing suddenly appeared in 1975. It was too late and too little. Twenty-five seats changed parties in the 1975 election, and the New Democrats were history. Transportation had struck again.

The vendetta carried out so effectively by Williams against the highways department probably stemmed from a long, drawn-out investigation that he had made of suspect land dealings by the sons of W.A.C. and Phil Gaglardi while that cabinet was in power. (The highways department was the authority to approve land subdivision in unorganized territory in those years.) From this nosing around, he earned the sustained dislike shown to him by most Social Credit party members (Socreds). It was unfortunate that, lacking the previous cabinet members as targets, he chose to take out his resentment on their long-suffering deputy ministers, who usually had nothing to do with their masters' misdeeds.[19]

Another source of Williams' dissatisfaction for the highways bureaucracy might well have been the dislike of many municipal officials in the Lower Mainland for the department's control of access to provincial highways. When Williams came to power, he made a telling comment that was reported in the media at Christmastime in 1972. He said, "When I get to thinking about all the power that has been given to me I could almost believe in anarchy."[20]

Wayne Richards, who was Williams' aide, and therefore a man at the heart of things, had this to say about the new government's behaviour toward the senior civil servants: "The NDP could have taken the civil service into their confidence, tried to involve them, and given them an actual sense of participation—approached them for help in implementing new ideas—but didn't. Instead it acted with suspicion and paranoia, trying to force things, to bludgeon them through. The civil service predictably balked."[21] Unfortunately Williams carried this management technique over to many of his cabinet colleagues, and many well-meaning deputies in the face of this became quite reticent with their ministers. He immediately accused them of withholding information, and it was from a minor example of this that he dressed down Tom Miard before a cabinet committee. One observer of this episode said that he too was shaking by the end of it. Miard, a fine public servant whose father was a renowned pioneering mines inspector at Fernie, never got over it; he soon went to an unhappy retirement. There were few men who aroused opposition to the new regime in British Columbia as Bob Williams did, and most of those who knew Tom Miard joined the forces against it.

One thing that Williams did right was to forecast that the very controversial Agricultural Land Use Act, restricting the development of arable land around municipalities, would result in soaring prices for lots unaffected by it. He recommended an excess-profits tax to accompany it. This was not forthcoming, and one organization to benefit immediately was the Canadian Pacific Railway, which received a multi-million dollar windfall when land it held in Vancouver was rezoned to meet an immediate need for residential and commercial land. It is intriguing to speculate why the New Democrats turned away from this.[22]

The horrendous forest fire on the outskirts of Kelowna in 2003 illustrated another adverse offshoot of this legislation. To avoid the Agricultural Land Reserve, developers spread out into the forest south of Kelowna. The Okanagan Mountain fire destroyed over 200 homes, many in the $1-million class.

It is said that when Barrett presided over the swearing-in of the first New Democrat cabinet in the history of British Columbia in the summer of 1972, he smiled constantly as if in a dream. On that cold day in December of 1975 when he impulsively called an election, the dream was over. The Barrett-Williams team had certainly exploited their short time in office to advance their theories of social democracy and unionism to the full.

## Chapter Five

## Mini-Wac and the Restraint Revolution: 1975 to 1986

*"Public sector workers cannot be in a privileged position and must be prepared to bear their share of the recession."*

*"Governments don't create jobs. Only the private sector can create meaningful work."*

—Premier Bill Bennett, summer of 1983

When Social Credit went down to defeat in August of 1972, its leader's age was the same as the last two figures of the year, and after a rather ridiculous attempt to rally the forces, he bowed to Father Time and resigned both his seat in Okanagan South and the presidency of the party. In the resulting by-election of September of 1973, his younger son was elected in his place. Two years later that son took his dad's erstwhile job as Social Credit premier and kept it for 10½ years.

William Richards Bennett was rather reluctantly compelled to run for political office by his rage at the new NDP government for its Agricultural Land Use Act, a measure that drastically restricted the development of arable land around municipalities and particularly Kelowna, surrounded by orchards as it was. Since the opening of the floating bridge across Okanagan Lake, the younger Bennett had become a very successful speculator in commercial buildings in Kelowna and in land both up the valley and near Westbank, across the bridge from his hometown.[1] In November 1973 the party held a leadership convention, and the son succeeded the father as the head of Social Credit. Bill Bennett went into the legislature as a rookie who was also the leader of the Opposition.

This inspired the NDP premier to make him the butt of much merriment. Barrett's performance at times in the House well merited one observer's comment that he acted like a stand-up comic impersonating a premier. Bill Bennett never forgot this embarrassment, nor did he forget that it was Alec Fraser (Fraser abhorred the diminutive

B.C.'s 27th premier (December 1975 to August 1986), William Richards Bennett's greatest transportation achievement was the Coquihalla Highway. He said that he could die happily when it was complete and that his dream had come true. Unfortunately, it turned out to be something of a nightmare due to the actions of his successor.

"Alex," much preferring to be called "Alec") and Don Phillips, the veteran members for Quesnel in the Cariboo and Dawson Creek in the Peace River district, respectively, who took him in hand and taught him the rules. When Bennett became premier in December 1975, he appointed both of them to the cabinet: Fraser to the highways and public-works portfolio, and Phillips to that of economic development.

There is a tradition, borrowed from the Mother of Parliaments in Westminster, that messages between members during a session in the House are conveyed by a squad of youthful pages who run around brandishing pieces of paper. Despite the best efforts of his tutors, before Bennett rose to answer questions from the House in his early days as premier, there was always a flurry of notes conveying their advice to him.

Alexander Vaughan Fraser, minister of highways from 1975 to 1986, could be quirky, stubborn, and totally infuriating to his staff at times. He abhorred intricate detail and was very poor at technical presentation; yet he earned affection and loyalty from all who were close to him. His approach to the Native population quickly broke down barriers. Premier Bill Bennett treated him at all times as a close friend and a respected elder.

Barrett was no longer there, but the surviving New Democrats had great fun mocking this practice, and this too was not forgotten by the new leader. From then on, he took pains to appear fully self-assured at the wheel and not assisted by others.

He demonstrated this attribute when he chose two civil servants—the highways deputy minister and the deputy minister of finance, David Emerson—to accompany him to a meeting of the four western premiers in the late 1970s. After a very tiring trip on a government plane to Thompson, Manitoba, these two were about to retire when they received a rather gruff instruction to report to Bennett in his hotel room late that evening. The premier had just received a copy of the agenda for the first day of the conference. He outlined the briefing that he wanted from each of them respecting the agenda, and he requested that they report to his room at 6:30 a.m. the next morning to go over that briefing prior to the meeting that was to start at 9:00 a.m.

The officials were rather disturbed when they realized that there was no meal service of any kind in the hotel at that early hour. When they arrived unfed the next morning, they were delighted to find that Bennett had arranged an excellent breakfast, buffet style, laid out in his room awaiting them; no small effort was required of him to arrange this late the night before.

Their curiosity at this man's motivation was further aroused by his instructions for the procedure that he wished to be followed at the meeting. He had been told that each premier would sit at a separate table with one of his staff on either side of him. Bennett demonstrated the hidden hand signals that he would use when he wanted briefing during the meeting, which was scheduled to be televised for most of the sessions. He told the deputy ministers that when either of them received such a signal, they should write their comments down on a piece of paper as if making notes for themselves. Then they were to quietly place that note on a pile of papers lying between them and the premier, for him to pick up some minutes later as if it were one of his own notes. The system worked perfectly and revealed the great lengths he was determined to go in order to prove he was not a man who was told what to say by his staff, a hangover from the shadow cast over him by Bennett Sr.: He wanted to bring more to his job than his name and kinship to the premier who outlasted them all, his father.

Bennett insisted that his two companions be included in a dinner put on for the premiers, an affair that they very much enjoyed. Each premier gave an after-dinner speech, and despite Bennett's reputation as a poor speaker, and despite his being in the company of several premiers renowned for their skill with words, he gave the best speech of all.

He was a man full of surprises. The people of British Columbia and his senior staff came to regard him like the "boy next door": They knew his face, they knew something about him, they knew his father, but they never knew him. Even so, he was often convivial, and he could be very socially acceptable, even charming and witty in small groups, as could his father, but he could not seize and hold an audience, or even amuse them, as Dave Barrett did. A spare, tense figure when he first came to the public stage, he had been an average student, refusing to go beyond high school. After that he became a workaholic, selling real estate when he was not expending energy furiously on the tennis court.

When he became premier, his wife accompanied him to Victoria and stayed there for a week or so for the purpose of finding a house for the family. She finally went back to Kelowna when she realized that she knew no one in the southern city and of course neither did their children; she returned to their house near the family enclave. For the 11 years of his premiership, Bill Bennett lived a rather monastic existence in an apartment in a multi-story hotel in the James Bay district of Victoria, relieved only from his work by rigorous sessions on the tennis court. He chose his friends carefully and exercised the maximum of discretion in his personal affairs.[2]

He soon showed that he wanted to excel in those areas where his father had, and road building and other transportation issues came to his mind quite early on. He eventually achieved success in his road program, but in his first term, he just put his head down and strove to renew the financial position of the province after the extravagance of the NDP. Road construction projects started up all over the province, but on a rather subdued scale—some in the Okanagan area, others in the north and on Vancouver Island. The railway scene was rapidly becoming disastrous, as the errors and futility of extending rail lines into nowhere, e.g., Dease Lake, became more and more evident. The new premier had to pick up the pieces. Only one new line was built in Bill Bennett's time, from a place called Tumbler Ridge westwards, as part of his northeast coal development.

On January 13, 1977, Bill Bennett made his first real flourish as far as highways were concerned. That was the day when the lieutenant-governor announced in the throne speech for the Socreds' second legislative session: "My government has directed my Minister of Highways and Public Works to proceed as soon as possible with the design and construction of a highway from Merritt to Hope through the Coquihalla Pass."[3]

It was to be a rather fateful move in respect to the younger Bennett's enduring reputation in the province. There were some reasons for this highway to be built over and above Bennett's interest in its benefit to his hometown, Kelowna. The highways ministry was most concerned about instabilities showing up in some of the rock faces near Hells Gate. There was concern as well about the need for an additional east-west route because of congestion on the Trans-Canada Highway on summer long weekends and the difficulty of four-laning through the Fraser Canyon.

Shortly after W.A.C. Bennett's death on February 23, 1979, the Social Credit Party won an election. They came out with 31 seats, four less than in 1975, and the NDP increased their representation from 18 to 26. The Liberals and Conservatives dropped from one each in 1975 to zero, some of this because of desertions from the old-line parties to Social Credit shortly before the 1975 election. Bennett picked up such experienced lawmakers as Pat McGeer, Allan Williams, and Garde Gardom, all of whom obtained cabinet positions, much to the disgust of many Socred backbenchers.

The verdict of political analysts was that these turncoats won the day for him in 1979, despite their stumbles along the way. Peter Hyndman had come over from the Conservatives in 1974, but proved to be not much of a bargain due to travel-expense indiscretions while on a visit to New York that were fully disclosed publicly. This was only the first in a succession of similar cabinet-member misdeeds. Jack Davis, for example, cashed in his first-class airline tickets, bought economy-class ones, and pocketed the difference.[4] Barrett jeered about these abuses after the election and also observed that only 32,000 more votes for his party would have swung the tide. He also made much of the fact that almost all of the legislation he had sponsored was still in place, particularly the Agricultural Land Use Act.

It could be said that Bill Bennett rather grubbed along through the last half of the 1970s, but in 1981 and 1982 the grub went into a chrysalis, and in 1983 he spread his beautiful wings and flew. That was the year he won his third mandate from the voters, this time with a little more authority. His party added 2 seats for a total of 35, and the NDP lost 4, to end up with 22 in a 57-member House. Bennett certainly did not accomplish victory without help. A retinue ranging from a makeup specialist named Nancy MacLean, who prepared him for television interviews, to a propaganda expert called Doug Heal, who specialized in television extravaganzas and highly imaginative brochures, did all that was possible to publicize his suitability to govern.

Then there was the "Baby Blue Machine," an offshoot of the Ontario Conservatives' "Big Blue Machine." This was his flying squad, led by Patrick Kinsella, known as the "best political hack in Canada,"[5] and supported by Jerry Lampert; both were professional campaigners and political managers. As well, there was his policy expert, the learned and trilingual Dr. Norman Spector. Bennett also had help from British Columbians behind the scenes—primarily from Hugh Harris, a real estate dealer from Kelowna who had organized Bennett's first campaign in his riding and acted as a general factotum thereafter, until his untimely death in April of 1982. He was the man who recruited Kinsella. And then there was Bud Smith, a lawyer from Kamloops, who was to become the commodore of the Coquihalla project. Collectively they nurtured the birth of the new Bill Bennett.[6]

One interesting and rather innovative aspect of this group from Ontario, true-blue Conservatives all, was their dedication to public polling. At a cabinet meeting held in partial seclusion in 1982, it was truly intriguing for a non-politician such as a deputy minister to hear the pollsters address the assembled politicians. The public's moods, concerns, and desires were likened to a supple tree branch swaying around in a changeable wind. The only way that they could handle this, they were told, would be by continuous polling, both by riding and provincially, to provide promises and remedies for the needs and fears of the electorate.

To poll and poll again was the way to electoral success, and the cabinet ministers in attendance obviously agreed. It was also hinted that the public memory was short and unrequited promises would soon be forgotten. Kinsella and Lampert were principals in Decima Research, a polling company that set up an office in Vancouver for the duration of the election. They were probably disappointed that Bill Bennett already had his own pollster, a man named Martin Goldfarb of Toronto, but they all worked along together quite amicably. Goldfarb's theory was conventional in nature, that polling results should be used simply to decide policy. Decima's persuasion was to another approach: They implied that these polls could be used to shape the public's moods and perceptions, which unfortunately conveyed an odour of trickery.

They all laboured to present the new Bill Bennett as a tough guy, quite different from the rather portly and cuddly teddy-bear image that Barrett had projected, and they obviously succeeded, bringing about a devastating setback to the New Democrats' hopes in 1983. Despite this, it could be said that Bennett did not win the election; rather, Barrett and his advisors lost a chance to return—mostly due to a lapse midway in the campaign, when Dave rather absentmindedly commented, "Yes, we will abolish restraint." This at once raised the spectre of well-compensated union workers returning to NDP public-works projects, while the rest of the populace suffered in the poor economy. Barrett ruined his political career right there.[7]

The strange thing about that election was that it was won on the basis of saving money rather than spending it, a new political philosophy called "restraint" (although there was $500 million set up for highways). Hard economic times had come suddenly in 1981, and the onset was so rapid and continuing that Bennett, who at first urgently pressed for an election for the fall of 1982, put it off at the last minute until spring, a better time for elections in B.C.

Also emergent after the Socreds' crushing success at the polls was the *éminence grise* behind it, another sinister figure, but a more lasting one than Bob Williams: This was a man by the name of Michael Walker, the free-enterprise champion of the Fraser Institute in Vancouver. He and it were to constitute a ghostly replication of the Kidd Committee of 50 years past. Kidd's philosophy could have been summed up as, "Protect the rich, do it on the backs of the poor, and to hell with the civil servants!" The Fraser Institute's approach was more sophisticated but in many ways similar.

In the face of the deepening recession at the start of the 1980s, Walker told Bennett that forest and mining revenues would just not be there in the coming years, and there would be no point in trying to save or maintain the social programs built up by the NDP. Strong stuff, and quite "Kidd-like"! He went on to say that the special-interest groups of the province were the major opponents of the capitalist system in B.C., and along with trade unionists, he rather surprisingly included doctors and lawyers among these groups.

He maintained that they all sapped the vital fluids of the marketplace and created social turmoil by their lobbies and protests.[8]

About the civil servants, Walker took no public position concerning Bennett's assault on them, which took place in the manner of the Kidd Committee's plans of the 1930s, but much more abruptly. Right after the election Bennett announced that there would be a 25 percent reduction in the civil-service complement and he indicated that this would not be all—not as bad as a 75 percent reduction of the budget to pay them, as had been put forward in 1930, but bad enough. History always repeats itself! Another fact that made things difficult was that B.C.'s teachers had gained a 17 percent wage increase late in 1980, at the start of the recession.

Prior to the 1950s numerous communities outside of the major cities in the interior of British Columbia and on Vancouver Island were largely company towns—townships and villages not necessarily owned outright by the companies (although some were) but dominated by them. These settlements were usually dependent upon a single resource, such as forestry, mining, or fishing. The city of Vancouver was the collection point for the products of these enterprises and was therefore highly dependent upon their well-being. This was the reason the catastrophic collapse of B.C.'s economy in the 1930s had such a dire effect on Vancouver when the demand for these resources disappeared.[9]

In the much less drastic recession that hit B.C. in 1982, a short-lived but quite drastic drop in demand for these same resources came to pass, resulting in a doubling of the unemployed in Kamloops, where a large mine closed down. In Prince George two pulp mills closed their doors, albeit temporarily, and similar job losses came about in other centres. When a brochure written by propaganda expert Doug Heal touting a job-creation project was issued during the campaign period, the total number of unemployed in the province was 126,000. In the next two months it rose to 193,000. B.C. was the worst-hit area in Canada, and the recession south of the border was not nearly as devastating.

There was a good reason that the recession was much less damaging in its effect than the one 50 years earlier had been. Excepting the external factors, it was largely because of W.A.C. Bennett's 20 years of endeavour. His goals of developing small entrepreneurial activities and improving transportation facilities in the province had triumphantly been reached. As a result of the improved ferry service to the Island and the improved highways in the Interior, the tourist industry in British Columbia had blossomed.

Throughout the province, small-scale enterprises were developing involving winter sports and summertime pursuits, including camping, high-country trekking, boating, and golf, etc. These brought visitors from elsewhere in B.C., as well as from the Prairies and from the United States. Manufacturing plants were appearing in such places as Kelowna simply because these were nice places to live. As well as this, the traditional Interior industries, such as wineries and orchards, were all growing steadily. Thus the dependence on the basic high-volume resources was lessened, and consequently, the vulnerability of the economy was diminished.

It might have been hoped that the younger Bennett would set aside politics in addressing all of this, but he did not. He was not the same man as his father because, despite his pollsters (or maybe because of them), he seemingly could not feel the true pulse of the public—at least not as a long-term heartbeat; maybe as an immediate fibrillation, but that was all.

In the glorious demise of his critics, his often hesitant self-confidence quite suddenly bloomed, and he confidently announced that his restraint program would bring about the most radical revolution in B.C.'s history. At the start of the first legislative session after the election of 1983, he tabled 14 bills dedicated to his radical revolution, and revolution he got.[10] It was called the Solidarity Movement, and tens of thousands of demonstrators took to the streets of Vancouver and Victoria. These bills were a good example of the exploitation of right-wing theories to the extreme, possibly the worst so far in B.C.'s history.

Half of the bills never passed and most of the rest were amended, and despite his successes, the departure of the 27th premier of the province was underway. His leaving was to take three years to complete, but after one year there were signs that he too saw the writing on the wall. In 1984 he proudly committed his government to the almost impossible task of building a 120-kilometre-long, four-lane highway across the Cascade Mountains, to be completed in the two years remaining before the opening of Expo 86, the world's fair to be held in Vancouver. This was Phase 1 of the Coquihalla-highway network, the Hope-to-Merritt section. He later added the other connections, adding up to 308 kilometres in all. It took him almost exactly 12 months to lose his restraint! One of the terminals of this highway extravaganza just happened to be close to his hometown, Kelowna.

In the interim, the civil servants of British Columbia had a lot of suffering to endure arising from Bill Bennett's short stage show, wherein he was cast as the messiah of the Fraser Institute. Among those suffering the most were many of the civil servants who had done so well for his father. The experience of one deputy minister at the height of the restraint tumult might provide some insight into what went on backstage.

One of the first bills to be passed was Bill 23, the Motor Vehicle Amendment Act, a regrettable piece of legislation rather disgracefully supported by the minister of transportation and highways (the name of the former ministry of highways and public works). Alec Fraser was the minister responsible for motor vehicle regulation throughout the province, but despite this, he had fought strenuously against mandatory seat-belt use, and he was now fighting equally hard against mandatory vehicle inspection throughout the province.

The scope of vehicle inspection was limited to the Lower Mainland and Vancouver Island, but the results were so beneficial and the service providing it so efficient, that plans were in hand to expand it throughout the province. That Fraser was opposed to its expansion was, ironically, because of its efficiency. As the member for the Cariboo, he was often beset by his constituents from far-off points in his riding. They travelled by pioneer roads whose many miles often shook off such things as tail lights and mufflers and disturbed such things as wheel alignment and ball joints—things that were very difficult to replace or to repair. The outspoken among these backcountry denizens wanted none of it. Despite the fact that a dusty road at night made tail lights even more necessary and good brakes and steering essential, Fraser chose to agree with them. Politics won out!

The struggle of the Solidarity Movement versus Bill Bennett went on all that summer. The premier was fortunate that the leadership of the B.C. Federation of Labour had been weakened by the death

## Bills prepared for the B.C. Legislative Session of 1983

**Bill 2**

The Public Service Labour Relations Amendment Act. This amends the B.C. Government Employees' Union's collective agreement. Essentially the union may only negotiate their wages, already controlled by the Compensation Stabilization Act.

**Bill 3**

The Public Sector Restraint Act. Provincial public servants may be terminated without cause once their collective agreements lapse. There is compensation, but seniority protection disappears. Most collective agreements expire on October 31, 1983.

**Bill 4**

The Income Tax Amendment Act. This removes tax credits for tenants and the elderly.

**Bill 5**

The Residential Tenancy Act. The rentalsman and his mediation services are removed effective Sept. 30, 1984. Rent controls are abolished.

**Bill 6**

The Education (Interim) Finance Act. Budget-making powers are removed from school boards in favour of the minister of education.

**Bill 9**

The Municipal Amendment Act. Zoning authority is taken from regional districts.

**Bill 11**

The Compensation Stabilization Act. Wage controls are extended indefinitely, and public sector wages may be reduced.

**Bill 19**

The Institute of Technology Amendment Act. Control of courses at the BCIT comes under the minister of education.

**Bill 20**

The College and Institute Act. Government takes over control of curriculum and board membership.

**Bill 21**

The Crown Corporations Reporting Appeals Act. Eliminates a legislative committee.

**Bill 23**

The Motor Vehicle Amendment Act. Wipes out government testing stations and discharges all staff.

**Bill 24**

The Medical Services Act. The government decides where doctors receiving medicare payments may practise, and makes it easier for them to opt out of participating in the Medical Services Plan.

**Bill 26**

The Employment Standards Amendment Act. Reduces employers' liability for wages when they become bankrupt. Eliminates the Employment Standards Board.

**Bill 27**

The Human Rights Act. The Human Rights Branch and the Human Rights Commission are replaced by a council appointed by the government.

of Jim Kinnaird, its revered leader, in February of 1983. The group inappropriately called "Solidarity" was less than that, consisting of two groups who were very uneasy marching together. They were the labour unions and a loosely combined amalgamation of community workers, the latter outraged by the legislation to abolish the human rights department and the office of the rentalsman. This strange body had been suddenly created and comprised two very reluctant allies.[11]

The most populous union in the province in 1983 was the B.C. Government Employees' Union (BCGEU), Bennett's major target, and its prominence was largely due to the erosion of industrial-union membership by the recession. It had been especially damaging to the International Woodworkers of America (IWA), previously the largest. Neither Art Kube, the new leader of the B.C. Federation of Labour (B.C. Fed), nor the BCGEU president Cliff Andstein proved to be of the mettle needed to face up to Bennett's shock troops, and the irritating mantle of leadership fell upon Jack Munro, the top man in the IWA. He was a fighter and well known to be that, but he was not sufficiently rounded out in experience and knowledge in this situation to do anything more than cope with it and try to find a face-saving way out of it.

Dave Barrett was the leader of the Opposition in the legislature, and he was the person in whom all resistance to this draconian legislation should have centred, but he performed so ineptly as to be embarrassing. He kept harping on details, such as the cost of Patrick Kinsella's furniture. While filibustering, he did manage to get dragged out of the legislature, from which he was banished temporarily. Despite this performance, his ineffectuality sealed his fate as the leader of the NDP.[12]

In November 1983, after a televised meeting between Norman Spector and Jack Munro, it was announced that the words "fairness will apply to any reduction in the workplace" would be added to Bill 3. The "fire without cause" clause would be removed and be substituted by wording about "alternate layoff criteria." Bennett and Munro announced jointly, also on television, that they had "reached an avenue for resolving their differences." The man from the woods put out the fire.

Bill 2 went into limbo, the human rights department disappeared, but a human rights council survived. The rentalsman decision was put off again and again, but the office finally disappeared. "Solidarity" collapsed, and Bill Bennett emerged as a winner, but not a complete one. He lost ground to the BCGEU on the "fire without cause" front, but gained when he successfully removed a "union labour only" dictate on the Expo 86 work then starting up. It came to a head when a non-union contractor named Kerkhoff was the low bidder on one of the first contracts. Bill Kerkhoff went to work, and the unionists worked alongside him as B.C. settled down uneasily, with a groan rather than a roar of rage.

The feeling about Bill Bennett that emerged from all of this in the minds of the people of British Columbia was rather like that which a man might have about his dog. When it barked, he would put up with it, but when it started to howl, he threw it out. The restraint program had not shown the proper restraint; this was the verdict indicated in the public opinion polls of May 1986.

Bennett announced his retirement on May 22 of that year, right after the triumphant opening of Phase 1 of the Coquihalla highway network, the 120-kilometre section from Hope to Merritt. This was carried out on time by the highway ministry, although it was done at considerable extra expense because of the deadline. Phase 2, the section of 80 kilometres from Merritt to Kamloops, as well Phase 3, the extension of 108 kilometres to Peachland en route to Kelowna, were all underway by then. This would make up the full 308 kilometres that would be Bennett's monument for future generations to enjoy.

He triumphed in the production of Expo 86, a most successful world's fair and a wonderful experience for the "good British Columbians," in Bennett's words, a distinction he apparently made for those who had not opposed restraint. He most graciously gave most of the credit for Expo 86 to its chairman, Jim Pattison, the multi-millionaire car salesman whom Bill obviously regarded as the best British Columbian. The "bad" British Columbians liked it too.

The promise to open Phase 1 by the start of Expo 86 had been met by the construction branch of the battered ministry of transportation and highways. They were helped by Bennett's assistant in the 1983 election, Bud Smith, who was now looking after the Coquihalla project. He had become the ministry's access to the heft of the premier.

Bennett's sudden resignation came as a severe shock to many, especially the members of his cabinet, to whom he sent an emissary to break the news. More surprised than anyone was Pat Kinsella, who had been convinced that Bill would fight strenuously in the upcoming election to continue his restraint mission. Kinsella had noticed, however, that after the Coquihalla opening Bennett had returned to his office and at once loosened his tie in the manner of the expression, "That's done!" He also had remarked that he could "now die happily."

Bennett said afterwards that he liked his hard regime of taking work home every night, sleeping, then working out for an hour or two on the tennis court at 6:30 in the morning, then heading off to work. He did say however that it restricted his social life; he must also have missed his family. Or could the reason for his retirement be that he and his mentor Michael Walker considered that he had shot his bolt sufficiently in the exploitation of their particular brand of free enterprise?

When he mentioned that he would remain as the member for Okanagan South, Patrick Kinsella asked jokingly where that was, and the premier answered, "Just follow the pavement!" Sad to say, his satisfaction with the achievement of this highway was to be short-lived, when the events described in a following chapter came to pass.

A truism comes to mind—when you build a monument, be sure that it is well founded on the ground, or at least that the ground around it has time to settle before you leave it, or an enemy may come along and push it over. Bill Bennett's major error, in respect to his final transportation achievement, was that he went away from the control of it too soon.

# Chapter Six

## A Fantastic Adversary: 1986 to 1991

*"To compare the estimates and costs of the Coquihalla Highway;*
*To find the reasons and justification for differences between*
*estimates and costs;*
*To examine other recent highway projects where costs may have*
*differed from estimates;*
*To investigate procedures for costing, administrating and reporting*
*highway projects;*
*To make recommendations."*
—Terms of reference for a commissioner's inquiry convened
July 31, 1987, by Order-in-Council 1546

The enemy, or maybe adversary would be a better word, for the man who pushed things over, was an individual named Wilhelmus Nicholaas Theodore Maria Vander Zalm. At least that was his name when he was christened into the Catholic Church, before he immigrated to British Columbia from Holland in 1947 at the age of 12. He and his family joined their father on a tulip-bulb farm at Bradner, B.C., a small Fraser Valley centre. The father had been in Canada on a sales trip in 1940 when Nazi Germany invaded the Netherlands, and he had remained overseas until the war's end.

The family had suffered privation in Europe under the occupation without their breadwinner, and the arrival in Canada must have been like entering another world. It was a world that young Bill was to attack with full vigour. Bill Vander Zalm shed the second, third, and fourth of his Christian names when he reached manhood, after trying the addition of Nick for a while, along with William.

After his marriage to Lillian Mihalic, Bill moved to Surrey, where they purchased Art Knapp Nurseries Ltd., and he settled down as an owner and a salesman. From 1969 onwards he served for three highly controversial terms as the Mayor of Surrey. In 1975 he became the Social Credit member of the B.C. legislature for that riding. He had shifted his provincial political bent quite quickly from the Liberals to the Social Credit party when his try at leadership of the former failed. He served in Bill Bennett's cabinet, but left under a cloud when he decided not to contest the 1983 election in Surrey. (More will be given on this later.)[1]

Bill Bennett's resignation as premier was also a resignation from his position as leader of the Social Credit Party. This required a leadership convention to pick a new captain for the ship to lead the party in the election planned for that year. The first point of interest in this exercise, called for July 30, 1986, was the venue.

When the senior management of Highways learned that the Social Credit Party was going to hold one of its most crucial meetings at Whistler, about 100 kilometres up Howe Sound from Horseshoe Bay by the winding Highway 99, they must have smiled. Their amusement would have centred on the history of this government with that place. Certainly Whistler was a wonderful asset to B.C. with its ski potential and the progressive realization of it; the peculiarity was how it all evolved.

For most of Bill Bennett's first term, from 1975 to 1979, hardly a couple of months went by wherein the promoters, and finally the mayor or members of council, of Whistler did not visit Victoria hat in hand. In a place where the value of building lots escalated at a rate faster than the skiers sped downhill as the ski runs were built, nobody seemed to be able to find the money to build a town. They were continually redirected to the highways ministry, who were directed to assist them. Such assistance included advice, services, and materials, all contributed at a "bare bones" cost. In this way, the town came into existence.

Then lo and behold, in 1983, at the height of Bill Bennett's restraint movement, Whistler received a Crown-corporation grant of $27 million as a bailout for its financial problems! It is noteworthy that in 1983 Bill Vander Zalm was the minister of municipal affairs. There was no doubt at all that the Socreds had chosen a place for their leadership convention where they had friends. In fact the only people in that town who were not happy with how it turned out were the winter-season, younger-set skiers and the hotel and restaurant help, who could not find affordable accommodations.[2]

The story of that convention, fascinating as it was, is not really in the purview of this book; however, events occurred there that are of some consequence historically. One of these happened before it even started and before Bill Vander Zalm terminated his period of indecision as to whether or not he would become a candidate for the party leadership (an outcome that many people in B.C. desired at that point in time).[3]

Right at the start the candidate openly stated that if he became the leader of the party and then the premier, he would have a problem with the life's work that he was currently working on. This was the creation of his Fantasy Garden project as a fully fledged tourist-oriented commercial attraction. He said that he planned to apply to the Agricultural Land Reserve Commission to have some of his lands released from the reserve and, in addition, that he would be applying to the municipality to have land reclassified to commercial status. If this took place when he was premier, it would be an obvious conflict of interest. This was without doubt the proper thing to do, and his problem was solved for him some time later on when both reclassifications took place.[4]

It was reported in the media that when someone asked the deputy municipal planner of Richmond how this came about, he said in amazement, "It just happened!" It was also estimated that some of that land might increase in value by an amount up to six-fold by this change. Vander Zalm later announced that he had conveyed the ownership to his wife, but nonetheless, when he became premier, indebtedness to his bank on behalf of the Gardens became a major embarrassment. This happened when he gave himself the finance portfolio, a part of his merry-go-round of cabinet changes; this one raised a rather substantial potential conflict of interest. He solved it by re-allocating finance.

That convention was also fascinating due to other surprising developments. Bill Bennett's favoured candidate, Kamloops' cowboy lawyer and Bennett's campaign director in 1983, Bud Smith, finally threw his votes to Vander Zalm instead of to Grace McCarthy, where everyone thought they would go. Bud had to wait several years before he got his reward, a cabinet post as attorney general.

Stephen Rogers was luckier. After saying he would never serve under Vander Zalm, he reneged and was appointed to cabinet immediately after the election, taking on several portfolios and eventually serving for a short time as highways minister. Jim Nielsen made the same vow, also reneged, missed re-election, and became the chairman of the workers' compensation board.

People like Alec Fraser and Kim Campbell, who either did not run or cast their votes elsewhere during the recounts, got nothing. Kim, who was prominent among the female membership of the party and was impressive intellectually, sealed her fate when she warned that "charisma without substance is a dangerous thing." Fraser was removed from the highways portfolio, which he had handled in good fashion under Bill Bennett for 11 years.

But a vision from the 1928 governmental change of power re-appeared. Instead of simply being known as the Vancouver business establishment, it was now called the "Top Twenty Club" (it actually totalled 60 members), all millionaires or close to it and all paying

$5,000 annually for the privilege of membership. All 12 leadership candidates had a closed-door meeting with the club membership shortly before the start of the convention, possibly right after Bill Bennett repeated his favourite practice of hosting breakfast.[5]

Vander Zalm ruled as unelected premier from August 1986 until the election on October 22. In that election, the total number of seats had been increased by 12; Social Credit won 47 seats in the 69-member House, the NDP 22. British Columbians truly thought they had a new messiah who would lead them away from restraint. In fact, he only led them into even greater chaos, and in five years it all came down on his head.

B.C.'s 28th premier (August 1986 to April 1991) was William Vander Zalm. His main effort in the transportation realm was to privatize the highways department. As minister of municipal affairs, he had brought SkyTrain to Vancouver and is due great credit for that and his later support of it.

His Fantasy Gardens was by then a multi-million dollar tourist attraction, complete with a replica of a Dutch castle—a copy of Captain George Vancouver's ancestral home in Holland—purchased by Lillian from the city council of Vancouver, who had used it at a downtown intersection to commemorate the city's centennial.

Bill Vander Zalm had been an outspoken critic of the Social Credit government in W.A.C.'s time, before his failure to gain the leadership of the B.C. Liberals, but when the 1975 election came around, he had decided to switch and obtained the seat for Surrey as a Socred. Never a backbencher, he had been immediately appointed to the cabinet as the minister of human resources by Bill Bennett. Flamboyant as ever, he soon made headlines with his "give them a shovel" approach to men on welfare. He was never a favourite minister with Bennett, and the latter sought to dampen his party popularity by keeping him in this dead-end position, but eventually had to move him to the municipal affairs portfolio in the shuffle of late 1978, because his popularity in the party had increased.

Bill Vander Zalm really took off in municipal affairs, acceptable as he was among the province-wide community of elected and appointed municipal officials. He had gained this acceptance from his Surrey mayoralty days, and he quickly built up a strong power base among the province's municipal leaders, especially those who shared his political style. He also acquired a deputy minister in municipal affairs who suited him: Bill Long, a civic administrator from Prince Rupert whom he eventually promoted into the chairmanship of B.C. Ferries. Vander Zalm was well liked throughout the higher echelons of government for his competence in cabinet-committee work, among his other administrative attributes. He of course kept up a strong prominence with the media.

One thing for which he never gained full credit was his initiation of a light-rail rapid-transit system for Vancouver. One day in the late 1970s, the B.C. deputy minister of transportation and highways was sitting in a meeting in Toronto when he received a phone call from the minister of municipal affairs in Victoria. The deputy minister was advised that arrangements had been made to fly him to Kingston, Ontario, where there was a test track for the demonstration of a fully automated transit system.

Vander Zalm, in his usual charming manner, asked if the deputy would be good enough to look at the system and make a report to him on it. The deputy did this and enthusiastically urged that it be adopted for B.C. This recommendation was taken forward by Vander Zalm and was accepted by cabinet, and Vancouver's SkyTrain came to pass. It remains as one of the province's finest assets in the field of municipal transportation, although it is regularly disparaged by the media, who consider it overly expensive.

But Vander Zalm wanted more than prominence in one agency of government. He soon came to the conclusion that the administration of all land owned or regulated by the provincial government should be in his ministry. This required legislation, so he prepared an act that would give him almost complete control of all the land assets of government, including many of those presently held by other ministers. Because he wanted to include the land for provincial highways and roads and arterial municipal streets, he quite understandably encountered the determined opposition of the highways minister and his staff. He also earned the opposition of the premier, as no first minister could permit such power to reside in one minister.

One move that Vander Zalm singled out in his desire for complete control was to abolish the Gulf Islands Trust, a thorn in his side in the blue waters of the Strait of Georgia, and it was the strong support for the Trust more than anything else that enabled the premier to bring about the demise of the proposed act. Bennett tried to achieve this tactfully, because of Vander Zalm's popularity in the party—he just let the act die on the order table. But this was not tactful enough. Vander Zalm was furious, and he burst out with his famous "gutless" remark about his colleagues in cabinet.[6]

He was then moved to the education portfolio; Vander Zalm without doubt saw this setback as the work of the premier and the highways hierarchy, and he decided not to run in the 1983 election. Rubbing it in even more was his embarrassing failure to be elected as mayor of Vancouver in 1984; his candidacy for this position was a sign of his desperation to return to the limelight. The final straw would have been the triumph of Expo 86, a wonderful lever to political glory, but the kudos had been casually passed by Bill Bennett to Jim Pattison—who was not even a politician! Bill Vander Zalm's advent to the province's highest elected office in 1986 finally brought him the increased power he had theretofore sought. The venue for him to exercise it,

Cliff Michael, minister of transportation and highways in 1986 and 1987, was a graduate of the Banff School of Advanced Management and a union-executive-turned-politician. About a year after he took office, he was involved in an incident at a cabinet committee meeting that led to his resignation. It seems that he had approached a businessman and attempted to sell him a lot in Salmon Arm. He probably did this absent-mindedly, as these meetings sometimes tended to make the mind wander.

in a reversal of positions with the former premier, turned out to be a highway well known to everyone in B.C. at that time, the Coquihalla, and Vander Zalm lost little time in putting the wheels in motion.

The first indication of trouble ahead was the revelation by the government in the House on July 16, 1987, that the Coquihalla had cost in excess of $600 million to date and that by the time Phase 3 (Merritt to Peachland) was complete, the total cost might be as much as $1 billion. This was announced by the highways minister at the time, Cliff Michael, the member for Shuswap.[7]

This was seized upon by some members of the press, who hazily recalled that the "Coquihalla Highway" at the very start had been estimated to cost $250 million and was now predicted to cost four times that. One television reporter burst out with the announcement: "Quarter billion highway costs one billion!"

The reason for the quotation marks used above around the words "Coquihalla Highway" is the confusion that was widespread in the media, both on paper and on television, about that highway project. Some news reporters never appreciated that the title "Coquihalla Highway," as first discussed back in 1984, then applied only to Phase 1 and Phase 2—from Hope to Kamloops—not to all three phases. The department did its best to keep things clear by always referring to the Merritt-to-Kamloops section as Phase 2, and the Aspen Grove-to-Peachland section as Phase 3 (this was later christened the Okanagan Connector). But some reporters never did get it straight and neither have some historians. (The map in Appendix A is of interest here.)

A very recent example is in *The Illustrated History of British Columbia*, published in the year 2001, where it is stated on the bottom of page 260: "The estimated cost of the Coquihalla was $375 million. By the time it was rushed to completion ... the cost would reach $1 billion."[8] The figure of $375 million was that used by Alec Fraser for Phases 1 and 2 in 1985. No estimate was ever put out for Phase 3.

The figure of $1 billion was never attained for all three phases. The final figures were $414.7 million for Phase 1, $155.5 million for Phase 2, with the cost of Phases 1 and 2 amounting to $570.2 million. The total cost for all three phases was $848 million. On Phases 1 and 2, it can be calculated that the overrun was 48 percent. This was bad, but much better than the widely held misconception of 167 percent—$375 million compared to a billion dollars, instead of $570 million. This misapprehension that the overruns on the Coquihalla highway were over three times what they really were was due to the above misconception, carried forward by the media and by historians, and the failure of Premier Vander Zalm to rectify this mistake right from the start. At the time of the inquiry he restricted all government contact with the media to his office. Unfortunately, a mistake like this, once enshrined, tends to be perpetuated.

A reading of Appendix A shows they could have justified the overruns in 1985. There is no doubt that Fraser knew the facts. His acting deputy minister at the time testified under oath that he told Fraser that the expenditure was $390 million early that winter on Phases 1 and 2. On the latter there were 16 projects underway at that time. There was only one on Phase 3.[9]

The Appendix contains a verbatim copy of a report given to Alec Fraser in September by his retired deputy minister, who was retained as an observer on Phase 1. This provides an estimate, as of the end of September of 1985, of $400 million for that phase only, and if the minister had reported this to the public, then he would have stayed out of trouble.[10]

But the decision was made, by whom it is not known, that they would carry through with their original estimates, no doubt hoping that the rosy glow of Expo in the spring and the triumphant opening of the magnificent Hope-to-Merritt highway would make all well. That is what happened, and they won the following election. All they had to do was to work a few multi-million-dollar special warrants through Treasury Board before the new fiscal year. Had there been an accommodating premier, it would have worked out fine; unfortunately for the reputations of both Bennett and Fraser, there was not.

After the election, the new leader of the Opposition saw an opportunity to embarrass the new government when the previous fiscal-year expenditures were finally laid bare. Bill Bennett was gone, but Alec Fraser was still around, albeit a backbencher by then and one who was far from well. In that winter he had his first operation on a cancerous growth in his throat, a condition that would plague him most cruelly until his death from it in 1989.

He took the blast from the NDP, and he got little help from his colleagues. Finally, it was announced that "An Inquiry into the Coquihalla and Related Highway Projects" would be conducted under the Inquiry Act, the order-in-council dated July 31, 1987. Concerning the "related projects," it seemed that the new premier had detected some inadequacies with the financing of the Annacis highway system, and he wished to throw that in. That part of the inquiry (which included the bridge later named the Alex Fraser Bridge, with the nickname Alec Fraser despised) was an added insult to the ex-minister and came to nothing.

What should have been done on the Coquihalla issue would have been to convene a bipartisan committee of the legislature, the usual way for such a situation to be dealt with, especially one that involved two administrations of the same party. For politicians, a commission of inquiry involving them is a major threat because it closely resembles a court trial in many ways, with a judge, witnesses, testimony under oath, etc., but of course without an accused, other than by inference— in this case the minister. Inferences are hard to fight.

With the wholehearted co-operation of the premier, the media was given full access to the commission. The commissioner did not call ex-Premier Bennett or the ailing Fraser, to the stand, but he did get the former finance minister, Hugh Curtis, to testify. He also got the former executive assistant to Bill Bennett, Bud Smith, who showed a complete knowledge of the highway and championed it quite adequately; it needed champions. Smith had been the link in the premier's office who had expedited changes and approved additions that had added substantially to the project's overruns.

The commissioner was as fair as he could be. He reprimanded the politicians at times, and he had some wrist-slapping for the civil servants, but many compliments too. The tragedy of it all was the lack of explanation, the lack of emphasis that the final achievement and the challenges that were overcome were what really mattered. The magnificent Coquihalla Highway should have been judged on what it was, not what it was supposed to cost and what it did cost. Above everything else, it was a magnificent piece of work.

Commissioner Douglas L. MacKay, P.Eng., was obviously a man fully familiar with civil engineering in the municipal field and with contract management in all its aspects, including estimating and scheduling, as were the experts he brought in from Alberta. His analysis of what was wrong with the Coquihalla project was naturally based primarily on these features. He was not a road-construction engineer experienced in the trauma of dealing with B.C.'s terrain, working in a short summer season above 4,000 feet, in a narrow valley, beset by numerous contractors, all frantic to make the best use of a few months of higher temperatures, with rain instead of snow. He could hardly be that, unless he had endured it, and he had not.

As he stated in the first paragraph of his report, MacKay had been granted the powers of a judge of the Supreme Court as provided in the Inquiry Act by order-in-council, but the fact that he had neither judicial knowledge nor experience was not a problem. The only witnesses to appear before him who could be assumed to be hostile were employees of the ministry of transportation and highways.

They were ordered to appear, and their legal counsel was a junior officer of the attorney general's department who was not permitted to speak on behalf of them at the televised meeting in Victoria, which lasted for several days. No contractors were summoned to appear, although they had been fully involved in the overruns.

The civil servants were naturally fearful for their careers, and their testimony was subdued and not at all aggressive. Their premonition about their jobs proved to be correct for many of them later on when Premier Vander Zalm, encouraged by the discredit in which the ministry was publicly placed by the inquiry, went ahead with its privatization immediately afterwards. *Sic transit* the organized expertise of the ministry in road-and-bridge maintenance and construction so evident everywhere throughout British Columbia. You seldom gain credit for denigrating those who are good people, and when Vander Zalm did this to Alec Fraser and the highways department, many in B.C. turned away from him.

Despite his criticisms, Commissioner MacKay was obviously sympathetic about the difficulties and problems so wonderfully overcome in the construction of the Coquihalla Highway, and he was quite outspoken in his praise of that in his report. His criticism was mainly concerned with the documenting and reporting of the ministry and the lack of modernization of these procedures. Of interest to many in the highways department was the mention of the ministry's contract documents. Many requests taken to Fraser to have these reviewed and modernized had been to no avail.

Alexander Vaughan Fraser seemed to have had an inbred reverence and awe of anything related to the parliamentary process. He got this from his father, John Fraser, who was the MLA for the Cariboo between 1912 and 1916 and the member of Parliament for that constituency in Ottawa between 1925 and 1935. He never made it into cabinet, either in Victoria or Ottawa, and that probably was why Alec held that rank in such reverence, particularly the office of premier.

While he never served under W.A.C. Bennett, Alec was the mayor of Quesnel for many years, and in that position, he had gained a most sincere and overwhelming respect for the first Social Credit premier that carried over to Bill Bennett. There was never a time, right up until the day he left office, when Fraser did not jump, visibly, when the red phone on his desk rang. It was on a direct line to the premier's office.

It did not matter that he had wet-nursed Bill Bennett into legislative politics in 1975; he never lost the fear—not of the man, but of the office. His policy as a cabinet minister was to stay back if at all possible, to never push forward unless he had to, and it showed. In the matter of contract documents his view was, "If they were good enough for W.A.C. Bennett, they are good enough for me." This mindset also showed in 1985 when he should have come forward and straightened the ship, but did not. In no way is this to detract from the goodness of the man or the kindness and consideration he always showed to all, especially with his wife Gertrude in their fostering of children and other good works.

Besides the good reasons for the overruns already described, there were others. In fact the engineers on that project were told by the premier's office (i.e., Bud Smith) to make it the best-ever highway, the safest, and the most environmentally suitable of all. That is why they installed descending lanes as well as ascending lanes along the flat bottom of the miserably steep avalanche-infested Boston Bar Creek valley—they went to six lanes there.

They carried the broad shoulders of the roadway onto the bridges, and they lavished concrete guardrail throughout. The decision to make the route a toll highway meant rebuilding already completed grade, out to 14 lanes of width at the booths. To illuminate the toll booths and the first-class camp they built for the toll-keepers, they brought a power line 30 kilometres up the Coldwater Valley. They used that to light up the 280-metre long snowshed and to heat the asphalt pavement in the transition areas at either end of it to prevent icing, and they also heated the pavement at the toll booths. They constructed numerous runaway lanes on the steep grades. Two explosive-delivery tramlines were built across the worst avalanche slopes to permit controlled blasting to prevent snow buildup.

The tollbooths took in $11 million in the first year of operation. When the motorists and truck drivers found out how good the highway was the next year, the traffic increased by 50 percent. In the year 2000 the toll revenue amounted to $42 million, of which toll-keepers expenses took away $1.2 million. The tolled section, Hope to Merritt, has now repaid its $415 million construction cost.[11]

To restore the fish habitat on these steelhead-trout rivers, ditch grids for spawning were built on flats in the valleys of the many tributaries, and special measures were used to treat riverbank protection to suit fish. Four-legged migrants had piped highway crossings built for them where needed. If this was Bill Bennett's error, it was a happy and productive one. It is a great injustice to its builders that it has not received the international acclaim it deserves.

And finally, before Bill Vander Zalm's reign went into its long death throes, one incident of highway contracting in his time demonstrates how easily and quickly politicians may fall into the role of the pot calling the kettle black. (This is all the more ironic because it features Vander Zalm himself, the man who pointed the finger so righteously at Alec Fraser for his misdeeds on the Coquihalla.) The circumstances take the ministry back 50 years and bring back the days of the small contractors of Pattullo's time—those men without equipment.

Vander Zalm's second minister of highways after he had pulled Fraser from the job, Cliff Michael, authorized a contract in the Lower Mainland to two low bidders who hired their dump trucks rather than owned them. It was not a small job, as they were in 1937; this contract was worth $19.5 million. Certainly the object of the exercise would be to hire gravel trucks at one figure and then to receive in excess of that from the government contract, and to attain this, it was necessary for them to keep hiring costs down, and they strove to achieve that—so much so that their hired truckers struck for higher rates. Rather than pay them, or hire others, they decided to wait them out, regardless of the terms of the contract, and regardless of the rage of the other contractors delayed by this.

Sonny's Contracting and Maximum Contracting, a joint venture, had been six months idle, and rather than have the bonding company reassign the contract, as the terms of the contract required, the Honourable Cliff Michael said there were "extenuating circumstances." He said that publicly, and he did not elaborate. When Bill Reid, Vander Zalm's tourism minister and the MLA for the area, was asked by the media if he was involved in this, he was more forthcoming when he answered:

"Did I talk to the Minister about the delay in the project? Sure, I talked about all the problems about the Richmond project. Mr Unger, of Maximum Contractors, is the best Socred supporter in South Surrey. He's a very good friend of mine and he's a constituent. I don't have any problem with that."

The reporter took the minister of tourism's comment to the new premier, who answered: "I don't know of any interference. I would do the same thing for a friend or a constituent." [12] A person with good hearing might have heard W.A.C. Bennett turning over in his grave. In the next session, Vander Zalm amended legislation to permit the negotiation of contracts.

On November 10, 1987, Premier Vander Zalm accepted Michael's resignation from the position of minister of transportation and highways, after Michael's admission that he had approached a West Vancouver businessman after a cabinet committee meeting the previous summer to talk about selling him some land. [13]

William Vander Zalm resigned from the position of premier of British Columbia on Tuesday, April 2, 1991, the day before Conflict of Interest Commissioner E.N. Hughes issued his report, which was highly critical of his actions. This report was described as "truly damning" by

Vander Zalm's successor, Social Credit cabinet minister Rita Johnston.[14] The commissioner's foremost opinion was that the premier had misused his position in the attempted sale of Fantasy Gardens.

Alec Fraser delivered his final speech in the B.C. legislature with admirable courage on March 9, 1988, with the aid of a mechanical device that replaced his vocal cords ravaged by cancer. Fraser was speaking against an allegation that he had misled the House in respect to the Coquihalla Highway. Soon after this occasion, he retired to his home in Quesnel, where he died on May 9, 1989. Alec had served in the Canadian army from 1942 to 1946 and had been elected as commissioner for the Town of Quesnel in 1949. His death ended 40 years of continuous public service. He was given a pioneer's funeral, with a horse and wagon carrying his casket, and the whole town turned out.

B.C. Conflict of Interest Commissioner E.N. (Ted) Hughes came to B.C. in the late 1970s, after he retired from the Bench in Saskatchewan. He worked for the B.C. attorney general's department and assisted the deputy minister of highways in dealing with the Westbank Indian Band for land to widen roads. The dealings were closely watched by Premier Bennett, a nearby property owner. Hughes proved to be reasonable, personable, and efficient in this and in a later, more prominent assignment.

His final address to the legislature was in response to a motion of the Opposition reprimanding the government for misleading the House over the expenditures on the Coquihalla Highway. Fraser's speech attacked the appointment of a commissioner of inquiry. The matter was one for the House, he said, and the House alone, and the commissioner was not a member of that House and was unknowing of its tradition, officers, and procedures. He believed that the matter should have gone to a bipartisan committee of the House, advised by the officers of the House, most importantly by the auditor general.

What were Bill Vander Zalm's errors in the way of transportation? Well, there were a few. Possibly the privatization of the highway ministry, which he undertook in 1987, would qualify in some people's minds, especially when he sold most of the equipment at fire-sale prices, but the jury is not fully in on that yet.[15] Another error might be the prologue to it: The downgrading (by incurring and not intensely refuting adverse publicity) of one of the finest highways ever built in B.C. would seem unwise. What Bill Vander Zalm thought he was doing when he called for a commission of inquiry into Bill Bennett's highway, instead of having it examined by a bipartisan House committee, is known to him alone.

By his failure to correct the misconception in the minds of the media and the public that the overruns on the Coquihalla project were more than three times as much as they actually were, Vander Zalm inflicted almost as much damage to the province's reputation in transportation matters, specifically highways, as a premier to follow him would in regard to ferries.

All of the above, or even a part, would fill anyone's list to the top, but the errors and exploitations in the field of transportation committed by Vander Zalm's successor and the premier after him would top them all.

For the final words on Bill Vander Zalm, a rather potent editorial in the April 3, 1991, issue of the Victoria *Times Colonist,* entitled "A Sorry Story of Stupidity, Conceit," suffices:

> Conflict of Interest Commissioner Ted Hughes, a retired public servant respected for his integrity, offered this particularly devastating comment on Vander Zalm's ethical ignorance: "Perhaps ... fundamentally, the premier's problem stems not just from his inability to draw a line between his private and public life, but in his apparently sincere belief that no conflict existed so long as the public wasn't aware of what was going on."
>
> Such a sorry legacy. There is a cynicism alive in the province today which will take able politicians many years to erase.

Sad to say, there is considerable debate today as to whether the people of the province have since then found sufficient able politicians and, more importantly, able administrators, to make this erasure.

## Chapter Seven

# The Nanaimo and Fast-Ferries Fiascos: 1991 to 1999

*"I would go out of my way to avoid having anything to do with Dave Stupich."*
— Premier Mike Harcourt's comment on the Nanaimo scandal

*"I have no expertise in managing projects."*
— Glen Clark, after he resigned as premier

Rita Johnston, the other MLA from Surrey, carried on for eight months in the wake of disaster, although the faith of this once-loyal cohort of Bill Vander Zalm was sadly shaken. During this time she committed no noticeable errors in transportation matters. The reconstruction of the Vancouver Island Highway continued, with the ministry of transportation and highways frequently updating estimates on the total cost of it and later on having no estimate at all, which was much safer. Generally it was excellent work, a lot of it by engineers from outside of the ministry, supervised by those of the ministry's highway design and construction staff who were left after privatization.

In October 1991 the inevitable election came around, and of course Bill Vander Zalm's exploits wreaked havoc, as history repeated itself and the electoral whale rolled over again. It was worse than when Barrett got crushed in 1975 and retained 18 seats. This time the Socreds had 7; in 1972 they had 10. The NDP won 51 seats, and the Liberals re-entered the legislature following a 10-year-absence with 17 elected members. Social Credit was well on its way to extinction. Once more the electors of British Columbia indicated that they really want no more than two principal parties to cope with and certainly not one that so blatantly endeavoured to force its philosophies upon the population at large.

When Rita Johnston became the 29th premier for a few months in 1991 (April to November), she was the ninth one who was also responsible for the province's roads. However, she was the first to become premier while already minister for roads; the others did it the other way around. She was a good highways minister, and when she replaced Vander Zalm, she kept the highways portfolio because, she said, she loved it. She did well with the Vancouver Island highway.

In the next election in 1996, Social Credit would shrink to one member, Cliff Serwa from Okanagan West, the last survivor.

Michael (Mike) Franklin Harcourt was the province's 30th premier (November 1991 to February 1996). Harcourt's name will always be associated with the Nanaimo bingo scandal. As a leader, he was usually described as accommodating and considerate, never appearing forceful. These were exactly the wrong traits to deal with the Nanaimo Commonwealth Holding Society situation. It is not always the best course to be a good fellow, especially when one is the premier.

Vander Zalm's misdeeds were terminal—everywhere but in W.A.C's back yard!

Mike Harcourt, who served as premier from 1991 to 1996, turned out to be an earnest but mediocre leader who tried to convert NDP members into liberals, without great success. His party was not helped by anything that he did, but rather by the support of previously centrist electors who were disenchanted with Social Credit because of the actions of Bill Bennett and Bill Vander Zalm.

Harcourt's major failing seems to have been severe political myopia as to what was happening with NDP party affairs in Nanaimo, where an erstwhile NDP finance minister of the 1970s, Dave Stupich, was outdoing everybody in financial skulduggery with his management of the funds of the Nanaimo Commonwealth Holding Society.

The criminal charges that were eventually laid in October of 1995 probably prompted Harcourt to put off the election originally intended to take place sometime between that fall and February of the following year. The allegations involved NDP party funds, which apparently had disappeared. In addition to this, if such were not bad enough, it was alleged that very large amounts of money had been taken from the returns of bingo games held on behalf of Nanaimo-area charities and misdirected away from them—not exactly the type of cloud any political party wants hanging over it in an election!

The Nanaimo Commonwealth Holding Society (NCHS) has a long history of political involvement. It was the vehicle used to

## The Exploitation of a Study

As a distillation of the exploitation of a mandate, there can be no better example than Glen Clark's treatment of a review of the privatization of road maintenance initiated by the Harcourt government in 1993 and published in a report one year later. (The review was chaired by a man named Peter Burton; the full title is in the bibliography.)

In the early days of 1994, Glen Clark was the minister of employment and investment, and he virtually controlled all road building within the province. His use of the study, which among other things, estimated that privatized road maintenance had cost the province $100 million more than what it would have for in-house maintenance up to that point, was the subject of an article that summer by well-known political columnist Vaughn Palmer. We are indebted to Mr. Palmer for his insight, no doubt gained from his contacts in the B.C. Road Builders and Heavy Construction Association, which includes the road maintainers.

Clark used this study in his dealings with the road builders. His position, according to Palmer, was that unless they agreed to have all contracts for the billion-dollar Vancouver Island Highway projects, which the NDP was going ahead with that year, be strictly for unionized employees only, the government would use this study as a reason to de-privatize road maintenance in the province. His gambit was totally successful: the road men caved in absolutely. Clark capitalized on this to gain higher wage rates for these projects, in addition to the added bonus of his increased stature with the unions.

During this negotiation, Clark kept the report to himself, and when it was released to the public some months later, it became clear the report was of no use for de-privatization. The review team said that they "did not support the option of simply reversing the privatization initiative by returning to the Ministry's original method of operation because this simple reaction would likely give rise to yet another round of excess expenditures." In the five years since privatization, maintenance expenditures in most road districts had doubled, which was why these companies were so loathe to give up their pot of gold, but Clark's approach precluded any discussion of this.

It was truly as in Vaughn Palmer's title, "Clark did it his way with highway report" (*Vancouver Sun*, July 18, 1994, p. A8). The whole exercise was an exquisite example of political interference into a governmental process.

reimburse Bob Williams when he relinquished his seat in Vancouver East to allow Dave Barrett, the defeated premier, to run in a by-election in 1976. Williams was temporarily tired of politics by then.

Among the specific charges laid against Stupich regarding the NDP and the NCHS were these:

- Committed theft and fraud against the New Democratic Party by transferring $18,037 held in trust by the society to himself.
- Committed theft and fraud against society by transferring $103,000 investment loss from Executive Mortgage Investments to the society for personal benefit.
- Committed theft and fraud against society by transferring $101,867 payable to the society to its deficit account.
- Committed theft and fraud against society by transferring $362,000 payable to the society by Marwood Services to himself.[1]

Premier Harcourt acted properly in preventing an RCMP withdrawal midway through, although he was accused by Liberal leader Gordon Campbell of trying earlier to cover up the scandal. Harcourt also acted correctly by tendering his resignation as NDP leader prior to a leadership convention that elected Glen Clark to that position.

A senior NDP party strategist summed it up in the fall of 1995 when he said about the fall election, "We have to wait until this is behind us." They did (narrowly), and in 1996 the NDP won again, this time with Clark at the helm.

Dave Stupich was convicted on some of the charges, but never saw the inside of a jail because of his incipient dementia.[2]

It was Harcourt and that premier-to-be, Glen Clark (Harcourt's minister

Dave Stupich, minister of finance for the NDP in 1975, astounded all who knew him casually as a government associate when the truth about him came out. Senior civil servants had always found him quiet and easy to get along with as a minister and MLA. Generally he was considered by them to be the last person imaginable to have committed the crimes he did.

responsible for B.C. Ferries in the early 1990s), who together made the first moves toward what would be the greatest errors in transportation in British Columbia's history. The first move was in 1995 when it was announced, without much fanfare, that a ferry terminal for B.C. Ferries would be built at Duke Point, near the Harmac pulp mill south of Nanaimo. Presumably it was built to relieve both the Departure Bay and Horseshoe Bay ferry-terminal congestion by starting up a route from Nanaimo to Tsawwassen, primarily for truck traffic. This would also relieve West Vancouver residents of that burden.

Fortunately (or unfortunately, according to how you look at it) there was land available at a commercially zoned building site, one that was put there many years before but never developed. This was Duke Point, a few miles south of Nanaimo just inland from the western end of Gabriola Island. The distance from Duke Point to Tsawwassen is 65 kilometres, compared to 54 kilometres from Horseshoe Bay to Departure Bay. (See map on p. 148.)

Few in B.C. realized what a profound move this would be in the evolution of the Strait of Georgia ferry crossings to Vancouver Island, and in fact what a gross error it was to build at Duke Point. To realize this, the reader requires knowledge from 20 years earlier.

The annual report of the minister of highways for the fiscal year 1972-1973 contains on page C 45, under the heading "Bridge Design," the following

B.C.'s 31st premier (February 1996 to August 1999), Glen David Clark's monumental contribution to transportation history was the fast ferries, as well as his promotion of the ferry terminal at Duke Point on Vancouver Island, when he was the minister responsible for the B.C. Ferry Corporation. This replaced the much superior site on Gabriola Island and it also made less probable a bridge to Gabriola Island, something that will come eventually. It is said by those close to him that Premier Clark was a great admirer of W.A.C. Bennett. It is a shame he did not replicate the qualities of his idol more effectively during his time in office.

### Well Paid Afloat

To understand the concerns of B.C. Ferries personnel about losing their overtime benefits, we can look at the contract brought about by the NDP government. The B.C. Ferries contract specifies that there shall be a 7½ hour day, and that after that, overtime shall be paid at double time.

This results in many of the crews, those on a route with scheduled overtime, working their last hours of the day over 7½ at these double-time hourly rates. The lowest paid, a galley helper, earns $40.36 per hour, and at the top of the list, a senior chief engineer (also a union employee) earns $80.54 per hour; the others fall in-between these rates. (The wage rates quoted are those at time of writing.) It should be remembered that overtime can also be required due to poor weather, heavy traffic causing congestion, delays, etc. This means that on a route with scheduled overtime of one hour a day, the galley assistant makes a minimum of $958.55 a week, and the engineer $1912.85—and of course considerably more on longer days. In fairness it must be added that all employees, including cooks and coffee-shop staff, must be safety certified by Transport Canada, and they are all assigned special duties in the event of onboard emergencies.

While this overtime rate is the worst of the contract items for any employer trying to reduce costs, other items in the contract also jeopardize efficiency. The most prominent of these is the requirement that promotions to supervisory positions be given only to employees with the longest service and the necessary skills, a poor substitute for merit.

On November 3, 2003, the union offered to allow flexible schedules—between 7 and 12 hours a day—without overtime being paid. They said this would eliminate all scheduled overtime, or overtime from unrealistic sailing schedules. They would not agree to overtime at time and a half, or to a change in the promotion rules.

statement: "Preliminary work was performed on structures crossing Dodd Narrows and False Narrows for the highway connection to the proposed ferry terminal on Gabriola Island."

This report was signed by the Honourable Graham Lea on July 31, 1973. But the work referred to had been carried out the year before, prior to the election of August, 1972, when the department was under Highways minister Wesley D. Black of the Social Credit Party, in the cabinet of Premier W.A.C. Bennett. Wacky Bennett had had the foresight to see that the place for the mid-Island terminal for B.C. Ferries to serve the Nanaimo area and north was Gabriola Island.

If his government had been re-elected, it is very likely that they would have gone ahead with the terminal on Gabriola Island. Of

The Horseshoe Bay Ferry Terminal was the main reason the B.C. Ferry Corporation built the "super speed" ferries, as they were first described. Three berths to handle three ferry routes—to Bowen Island, the Sechelt Peninsula, and Vancouver Island—were all served from this small waterfront jammed between the marina in the forefront and the steep cliffs in the back.

The double-deck structure designed to increase the pre-boarding area for waiting vehicles was just begun when this picture was taken in 1968. Even when the double-deck compound reached its full capacity of 816 "automobile equivalents," traffic waiting for ferries at busy times stretched back to occupy the curb lane of the four-lane Trans-Canada highway on its steep approach to the landing.

The theory behind the fast ferries, which were to travel at twice the speed of the vessel shown, was that if the ferries on the most popular route (to Nanaimo) left more often, then the number of cars waiting for that ferry would be reduced and the overcrowding of the terminal thereby eased. The congestion was greatly helped in the mid-1990s by the introduction of a route, for trucks primarily, from the Tsawwassen terminal to a new terminal at Duke Point near Nanaimo. But the congestion at Horseshoe Bay still remains.

course, if the Horseshoe Bay-to-Nanaimo ferry service had been abolished, the designation of the Second Narrows Bridge-to-Horseshoe Bay section of highway as part of the Trans-Canada Highway would have become meaningless; another route for the Trans-Canada would have had to be designated. This route would probably have led to the new terminal in Richmond and from Gabriola Island to Vancouver Island, to rejoin the previous route south of Nanaimo.[3]

After Barrett became premier in 1972, it took several months for someone in his government to eliminate this project totally. The annual report for the next fiscal year contains no mention of it anywhere. Work continued until May of 1973 until the axe fell and

Wesley Drewett Black, minister of highways from 1968 to 1972, succeeded Premier Bennett in the post. He gave the ministry what Gaglardi had not provided in the last few years, his full attention and a genuine interest in open co-operation with the staff. A perfect example of a team player in cabinet, Black held four positions: highways, provincial secretary, municipal affairs, and social welfare. He certainly would have built the bridge to Gabriola had he remained in office.

then the project just disappeared. The work included a hydrographic survey and preparations to construct a marine model to study current effects. Presumably it was buried deep in the files.[4]

At the same time, similar action was taken regarding ferry terminals to match on the mainland. This was an investigative design project undertaken for highways, under the title "B.C. Ferries—Route II—Proposed Ferry Terminal. Alternate Sites" carried out by Swan Wooster Engineering Co. Ltd., a Vancouver company. Their job was to come up with alternate ferry terminal proposals for the mainland to be located somewhere immediately across the Strait from Gabriola Island. There were four proposed sites contained in their initial report, two on Iona Island (North Arm and Iona jetties), one on Sea Island, and one at Steveston.

The North Arm jetty site was much preferred by the consultant, because it was the one most removed from the Fraser River. The first site on Gabriola was to be on Sear Island, which would be connected to the larger island by a bridge. This proposal was vetoed by the politicians because it was alongside the Royal Vancouver Yacht Club's Tugboat Island, and a site close to Breakwater Island was chosen. The new crossing would be half the length of the existing one.

Of course Dave Barrett and Bob Strachan, his minister of highways, had a dilemma in 1973—how to tell the Nanaimo ferry workers, among their strongest supporters, that they were going to cut their work hours in half. They avoided that problem by vetoing the shorter route, and B.C. Ferries and the highway department had to make the best of it for the Nanaimo route by ordering three new ferries capable of 19 knots—three knots faster than the old ferries—and building another berth at Departure Bay.

A ferry worker's shift included two round trips of 116 nautical miles, plus loading or unloading time of 25 minutes. Even with the speeds of these new vessels, a full-day shift for the Nanaimo route had to be at least 8½ hours and realistically, 9 hours or more, thus ensuring the crew at least one hour at double time daily and often more. Later it officially became a scheduled overtime route. So Barrett got smiles instead of brickbats from the ferry workers.

In April 1974 the jurisdiction of the B.C. Ferries Division was transferred to the new department of transport and communications; however, the design, construction, and maintenance of the B.C. Ferries terminals remained with the department of highways. The Gabriola terminal proposal of the 1970s was laid aside. Dave Barrett's planning for the future did not extend further than the next election. This was a prime example of a premier exploiting his mandate by taking action in favour of the few, to the detriment of the many, i.e., the people of central and northern Vancouver Island. (The proposal is still there of course, even if it is now very far back in the files.)

Then came Bill Bennett. Initially he was too busy finding funds for immediate problems caused by NDP spending to consider new ferry routes, and then of course came restraint. Finally, young Bill became too immersed in his Coquihalla project to have any interest at all in a major undertaking on Vancouver Island. In the interim B.C. Ferries became a Crown corporation, and on October 1, 1985, that corporation took over dock-engineering operations, not only for its own terminals, but also for the coastal ferries of the ministry of transportation and highways, whose ferries it acquired (much to its later regret). Despite this, however, when Transportation and Highways Minister Neil Vant authorised "A Transportation Planning Overview for the Province of British Columbia" in 1988, the engineers and planners obviously had before them the plans of the Gabriola site. This report, issued by the Delcan Corporation in October of that year, contains the following statement on pages 14-5 and 14-6:

"The Ministry has been lobbied in recent years by a private developer for a bridge from Vancouver Island to Gabriola Island. In addition to this, it has often been suggested that a third crossing from Vancouver to Vancouver Island will be required at some time in the future.

"This new crossing, depending on its location, could make the Vancouver-Nanaimo run up to 24 km. shorter. The required access to Gabriola Island could be connected to Highway #1 and therefore provide a much more direct route to the ferry terminal than is possible at Departure Bay with its present street systems and traffic signals. It would especially tie in well if there was a Nanaimo bypass.

"The shorter run would reduce operating costs and travel time considerably. However it would require construction of two new terminals and the associated road infrastructure at each end. The Gabriola and Vancouver connections would be expensive. These costs would have to be balanced against using larger super ships on the existing routes in the future. If the existing fleet is maintained, the older vessels will have to be refurbished and this will be a considerable cost. If new super ships are constructed, they too will be expensive and the difference between refurbishing and buying the new super ships would be compared against the cost of the infrastructure required for a third crossing.

"The third crossing is controversial on both social and environmental grounds and the opinion is equally divided between proponents for and against."[5]

Neil Vant, minister of transportation and highways in 1988 and 1989, was a lay preacher from the Cariboo and the second member for Alec Fraser's riding. Vant was unsuitable for the highways portfolio, and Premier Vander Zalm finally requested his resignation over an incident in cabinet. Vant took over from Stephen Rogers after Rogers privatized the highways department. He submitted to Vander Zalm's domination of the situation.

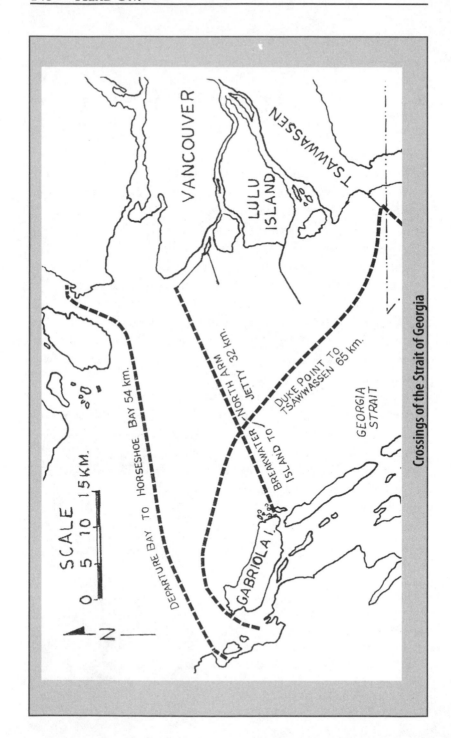

Crossings of the Strait of Georgia

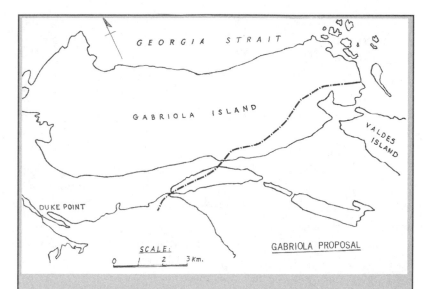

## Terminals on Gabriola Island and the Mainland

In the years 1972 and 1973, the dock-design engineer of the B.C. department of highways submitted proposals to solve the anticipated inability of B.C. Ferries' Horseshoe Bay-to-Departure Bay ferry run to meet future traffic volumes.

The proposal submitted to B.C. Ferries was to build new terminals at Gabriola Island and on the mainland. There were four alternatives on the Vancouver side: at the end of the North Arm jetty, at the end of the Iona Island jetty, at the end of the Steveston Jetty, and on the south side of the confluence of the Middle Arm of the Fraser River. These would involve causeways of up to four miles in length. The mainland proposals were conceived by Swan Wooster Engineering Co. Ltd.of Vancouver, B.C., whose preference was the North Arm Jetty site. The new terminals were estimated in 1973 at $25 million each. A bridge and road to Gabriola Island would also be necessary. The planning and design of these were undertaken by the department and then abruptly cancelled in the summer of 1973.

## Crossings of the Strait of Georgia

The map opposite shows the existing routes across the Strait of Georgia from the Nanaimo area and the route that would be possible with a terminal on Gabriola Island located near Breakwater Island. For better movement in and out of that area, double-ended ferries would be preferable. Not shown in full is the crossing from Tsawwassen to Swartz Bay, which scales out at 41 kilometres. In the event that the Gabriola terminal is built but the North Arm Jetty terminal is not, the distance from Breakwater Island to Tsawwassen scales out at 44 kilometres. All these distances over water are approximate.

What Neil Vant did with this report is not known, but probably it was very little. The Reverend Vant, the second member for Cariboo, did not stay long in the job. He was as ineffective as Cliff Michael, who had also departed under a cloud within one year as turmoil surrounded Premier Vander Zalm. In any case, nothing happened about the Gabriola terminal proposal in 1988.

Here the removal of the highway authority from the overall planning of ferry crossings by Bill Bennett in 1985 is crucial. It took away another point of view and put all the decision making about terminals into the board room of the B.C. Ferry Corporation and, more importantly, with a board of directors who relied heavily on the senior officers of the corporation. They were primarily "ship" men and certainly not up to a confrontation with the people of Gabriola Island. Did the words "super ships" stand out for them in the report, perhaps alerting them to dire consequences later on?

The key decision was made by Premier Mike Harcourt in 1995, presumably on the recommendation of Glen Clark, his minister responsible for B.C. Ferries, to build a terminal at Duke Point. How much fully informed public discussion there was about that is not clear—certainly there was not much outside of the Nanaimo area. This was a much easier undertaking to achieve than to build on Gabriola Island. The land was already all set up and suitably zoned. By building at Duke Point, the Gabriola proposal was put on the shelf, well and truly.

The crossing from Duke Point to Horseshoe Bay or to Tsawwassen is fully as long as that from Departure Bay to either point. Duke Point was simply an easy-to-build terminus for one more long ferry route to the mainland. The demise of Gabriola as a short-route terminus across the Strait of Georgia is therefore the responsibility of all these premiers—Dave Barrett, Bill Bennett, Bill Vander Zalm, Mike Harcourt, and Glen Clark (when he was a minister). Rita Johnston was not in the premier's chair long enough to merit blame.

In 1994 Premier Harcourt and his minister for B.C. Ferries, Glen Clark, jointly announced that three totally innovative vehicle ferries would be built for the Nanaimo-Horseshoe Bay run. These were to be aluminum-hulled vessels of 250-car, 1,000-passenger capacity, and they would move at speeds of 37 knots (70 kilometres) per hour. The initial estimated cost for all three was $210 million; they ended up costing more than two times that amount. In comparing vehicle-carrying capacities, the conventional "Spirit Class" ferry on the Swartz Bay-Tsawwassen run carries 470 vehicles and 2,100 passengers at about half the speed.

The ferry corporation has always had a problem maintaining an hourly summer service on Route II, Nanaimo to Horseshoe Bay, because of its length. It is 29 nautical miles, compared to Route I, Swartz Bay to Tsawwassen, which is 21.9 nautical miles. Route II certainly required (at least) Cowichan-class vessels capable of a service speed of 19 knots in order to perform adequately on this route. Faster ferries were always needed for the Nanaimo run.

The new vessels were to be catamaran style, and at 122.5 metres in length, they were destined to be the largest catamarans, less one, in the world. Unfortunately, because they would have to use the existing docks, they could not be true catamarans in their dimension. They were built by Catamaran Ferries International Ltd., a company formed by the province. The term "Pacificat" was created to publicize them, along with a painted cat on the hull.

In the mid-1990s Glen Clark, the minister in charge of B.C. Ferries, decided to build three "super ship" ferries in an attempt to solve the traffic problems of Route II, Nanaimo to Vancouver. Only two of the three vessels produced went into service, but these were soon taken off the run because they were unsuccessful. The *Pacificat Explorer*, shown here, was one of these two. The reported cost for all three was $463 million.

The first of the new ships was launched on June 21, 1998, two years behind schedule and $16 million over budget. It was named the *Pacificat Explorer*; it went into service in July 1999, and in no time at all the troubles really began. These were horrendous. An inability to handle large trucks or large recreational vehicles was the first fault noticed, followed by an almost complete failure to maintain the vaunted speeds, due to a lack of engine power and reliability.

There was also an outburst of protests from seaside residents on Howe Sound from the gigantic wash created by the huge ferry's wakes. Huge fuel consumption, hull corrosion and cracking, blocking of intakes by floating debris—all of these happened, while the passengers added to the furore with complaints of poor accommodation, uncomfortable seats, and lack of space. The customers much preferred the older ferries, and they said so. These "fast ferries" were hard put to keep up with the slower ones.

When the second ship, the *Pacificat Discovery*, came on the scene, there was no difference. It was taken out of the water for repairs three days after its maiden voyage, and the once-proud B.C. Ferry Corporation was hugely embarrassed shortly after that by having to take both of its newly built fast ferries out of service permanently after trying, half-heartedly, to use them part-time. The third fast-cat, the *Pacificat Voyager*, never went into service at all. It sailed directly into storage at the B.C. Ferries Deas Dock and was put up for sale along with the other two.

The announcement that all three were for sale was made in March 2000, along with the stunning news that each had been slashed in book value to $40 million. The whole exercise of building these misbegotten vessels cost $463 million, for which the B.C. taxpayer and ferry user got nothing other than trouble, and three apparently unsellable, unusable ferries. Had they been sold at book value (they were not) the corporation would have lost $343 million, plus much more in loss of reputation, but in the end it wound up losing many more dollars than that. For an example of an error by a premier, this beats them all![6]

As mentioned earlier, the map "Crossings of the Strait of Georgia" shows that the distance from Gabriola Island to the proposed terminal sites is 30 or 32 kilometres, whereas the crossing from Nanaimo to Horseshoe Bay is 54 kilometres. It is not difficult to conclude that had the conventional ferries been put on the shorter run, in effect they all would have been converted to fast ferries—without the extra wear and tear, without the additional huge fuel costs, without the extra employee time and costly new technology, and especially, without the wash on the beaches.

Here of course the politics of exploitation that burdens British Columbia came into play. It is almost certain that unionized employment on the ferries was in the mind of Premier Barrett when he made his decision about the Gabriola terminal. With Harcourt and Clark, a similar objective came to the fore with regard to the fast ferries. Concerning union matters, only one feature seemed worthwhile: This was the high-tech employment and experience gained on aluminium-hull construction. Unfortunately, it was not done successfully. Certainly, the Australians who excel at it were not about to give away their secrets to another country.

Were all those hundreds of millions of dollars wasted on the fast ferries and those poorly applied to the Duke Point terminal worth the safeguarding of ferry workers' jobs? Did Bill Bennett or Bill Vander Zalm listen to the critics of the Gabriola proposal among their political supporters without considering the population at large?

Will any premier of British Columbia look at the ferry problems of Vancouver Island and its nearby smaller islands in the long term and spend a few million to offset continuing ferry costs? Will they look at connections, wherever possible, by bridges? The only one done to date is the bridge between North and South Pender. A road-and-bridges solution is feasible between Mayne and Saturna via Curlew and Samuel islands, as is one from Gabriola to Valdez, in conjunction with connecting Gabriola to Vancouver Island.

This type of solution, with the help of some fairly large bridges, has been achieved in Washington state—a place where politicians seem to come into office quietly and run things as well as possible for all the people, instead of exploiting their own particular political theories. (Another striking difference in how things are done there is the state law stipulating that their ferries must be built in Washington state.) But any talk of a bridge or tunnel across the Strait of Georgia, with the techniques available now, is premature and pointless. Such a crossing should await a demonstration of feasibility, and the start of a structure across the Straits of Messina would be a good indicator. A project to design a crossing for these straits has recently been announced.[7]

In respect to this, on December 17, 2002, the ministry of transportation and highways issued a statement on a report prepared for them entitled "A Potential Fixed Link to Vancouver Island." The report maintained that cost-effective technology to build a bridge connecting Vancouver Island to the mainland was not yet available. With current technology, the report writers estimated that such a structure would cost $12 billion and take 25 years to achieve. On a 20 percent return, a user could expect to pay a one-way tariff of $800. Options that were considered included a bored tunnel, a floating tunnel, a pontoon bridge, and a multiple-cable-stayed span structure with floating piers. One major obstacle to the 26-kilometre crossing in water up to 365 metres deep is the earthquake hazard; there have been 13 major earthquakes of 4.9 severity or higher since 1909. Conditions on the sea bottom present further obstacles, with up to 450 metres' depth of soft sand and marine-slope instabilities that can trigger underwater slides on the Strait of Georgia's eastern shores.

It may be that the time has come and gone for another full-size terminal on the Vancouver side, such as at one of the four sites described previously, and unfortunately, this is probably also the case for Gabriola. However, there is an alternative that could make a huge contribution to the transportation of passenger traffic from Vancouver Island to the mainland.

This would be a passenger ferry service running from Gabriola to Point Grey. To minimize the effect on Gabriola, the parking lot at Duke Point could be used by eastbound passengers to park their cars and then travel by bus to Gabriola. There would be bus service to either terminal, to Nanaimo on one side and to downtown Vancouver, or Vancouver airport, on the other. Future extensions of SkyTrain to Point Grey or the Vancouver airport would also be of great value if they were included in this plan.

This would necessitate road access to Gabriola by a bridge, which is needed in any case, and at the same time it would save the island from an invasion by ferry-bound automobile or truck traffic. It is quite feasible that the trip from Nanaimo to downtown Vancouver or to Vancouver airport by this arrangement could be achieved in less than two hours, using a high-speed passenger ferry, which is about half the time that it presently takes through Horseshoe Bay. The real message here is, "If the people cannot have the best car ferry system, at least give them the best passenger service!"

Of course, if the speed of the fast-cats were reduced to 20 knots instead of 37, if the kitchens and restaurants were removed to give more and better short-trip accommodation, and if only cars and light trucks were allowed on, they could very likely have given wonderful light-vehicle service from Gabriola to Point Grey. They would be much better off landing at Sear Island, but would the people of Gabriola and the members of the Royal Vancouver Yacht Club permit that?

Summing up the overall situation, a solution to the Nanaimo-run problems was presented to Premier Dave Barrett in 1973, and he passed it by, presumably for political reasons. Then the next two premiers, Bill Bennett and Bill Vander Zalm, aware as they must have been of the problems of the Nanaimo run, procrastinated.

Finally one premier, Mike Harcourt, was persuaded by his ferries minister and the ferry directorate to build a port at Duke Point and to start constructing super-fast ferries. This was supposed to be the final solution, and of course it was a spectacular failure, at least as far as the ferries went. The Duke Point terminal and the run from Tsawwassen solved the West Vancouver truck-traffic problem, all of this at a high cost in ferry operating mileage. The Nanaimo traffic problem was solved by the bypass. The obvious but politically difficult solution to the Nanaimo connection, to shorten the route by building on Gabriola, was carefully kept away from public discussion.

As another possible move, the Vancouver-to-Victoria route might be cut from a 44-kilometre sea crossing (Tsawwassen to Swartz Bay) to a 28-kilometre crossing (Tsawwassen to Long Harbour), if a bridge were built across Sansum Narrows to Saltspring Island, and a terminal established at Long Harbour. This would be a very expensive undertaking and would likely involve tunnelled approaches; it would be highly disruptive, and the balance presently points against it.

In reading this chapter, the bemused reader may ask, "What does the Nanaimo bingo scandal have to do with transportation?" The answer is that the government of Mike Harcourt in 1994 and 1995, amid a growing groundswell of suspicion rising up about these goings-on in Nanaimo, found itself in desperate need of a diversion. What better cure than a solution to the area's highway and ferry problems with the bypass, a new terminal at Duke Point, and talk of these wonderful new ferries?

The last act concerning the fast ferries took place on March 24, 2003, when all three ferries were put up for bids at a no-reserve-price auction in Vancouver. The winning bid for each of the three vessels was that of a Vancouver-based organization known as the Washington Marine Group, a subsidiary of which, Vancouver Shipyards, was a leading member of the consortium of companies that built the fast ferries. Ironically, during the construction phase, Washington Marine had offered to purchase the ferries it was helping build for $210 million, and then lease them back to the B.C. government.

There were seven bidders from around the world. The total winning bid for all three vessels was $19,240,000, approximately four cents on the dollar when compared to the original $463 million cost of them to the B.C. Ferry Corporation. Asked what he would do with them, new owner Kyle Washington indicated that another subsidiary, Seaspan International, a world-class tug and barge company based in Vancouver, "could find a use."[8]

Suffice it to say that to those in government who have dealt with the British Columbia shipbuilding industry over time and its constant pleas for special treatment, there are ironies in the above almost beyond belief. The one good thing about the final scene of this comedy of errors is that as far as it is known at time of writing, these three hulls will remain in British Columbia. Their value far exceeds the scandalously low price paid for them, and the province's citizens will surely scrutinize their future use—after all, they have a very large interest in them! As William Rayner outlines in his book, *Scandal!!*, there were three NDP premiers involved in this ultimate folly originating in the Belleville Street office of the first minister. They were Mike Harcourt, Glen Clark, and Dan Miller.[9]

In closing, it is only fair to list the achievements to the greater good in transportation that transpired in the years following the first Bennett. The second Bennett, of course, achieved the Coquihalla Highway, without doubt the best highway in the history of the province and certainly the one that has generated the most revenue in dollars. As mentioned, the successors to the Bennetts did well with the Vancouver Island Highway, despite the NDP's scandalous insistence that union wages for contract work on projects such as this be increased over those paid on other projects.

Then there is SkyTrain, essentially Bill Vander Zalm's project from the outset. Phase 1, from 1982 to 1986, took it from Vancouver to New Westminster and was completed under Bill Bennett, initially guided of course by his minister of municipal affairs. Phase 2, 1986 to 1989, took it to North Surrey, and Phase 3, 1989 to 1994, into the municipality's town centre, partially under Vander Zalm and then the NDP. It now extends even farther. Besides this, the NDP instituted two other projects: one was Seabus, a ferry service across Burrard Inlet. The brainchild of Dave Barrett, it was started in 1975 and completed by 1977. The other was the West Coast Express, the first British Columbian commuter rail service, put in place between 1994 and 1996. All of these are excellent transportation projects brought to the people of the Lower Mainland. The NDP deserve great credit for extending SkyTrain; it is a significant benefit to its users, allowing them to move quickly through the automobile-choked environs of Vancouver.

All of these undertakings show that social and environmental effects can be offset in favour of projects that are for the greater good, and the realm of transportation is a key sphere. The greater good has had rather a rough ride at times throughout the years at the hands of our premiers and their errors and exploitations.

British Columbia enjoyed a fine reputation internationally for its highways and ferry system prior to two events. After the commissioner's inquiry into the Coquihalla, with its resultant media furore and uncontested reporting of non-existent gross overruns, and the fast-ferry fiasco, that reputation has dimmed, but hopefully only temporarily.

Speaking of B.C.'s future reputation for highways and ferries and the management of such, there still exists a traditional engineering excellence that has now largely moved from the civil service ranks to those of private industry. It has prevailed with the Vancouver Island Highway, and it will be there when the Squamish Highway is taken on. In the matter of the ferries, recent events offer some hope that the old practice of filling Crown corporation boards with directors whose qualifications comprise small-scale political prominence and little else might finally become a thing of the past.

On April 2, 2003, the B.C. government announced that the Crown corporation running B.C.'s ferries was on the way out, and that a private company would be formed, somewhat on the lines of those managing B.C.'s airports. Safeguarding itself for the next election, the government also stated that the present service levels and routes and low rates of fare increases would be sustained for at least the next five years. The intention to build new but conventional large Spirit-Class ferries was also announced. Maybe those at the highest levels of supervision will at least, and at last, have a majority of individuals among them who know something about what they are appointed to oversee.

To many of its readers, this book might indicate that the people of British Columbia would be much better off it there were a buffer of some kind between their premier and their transportation system. This could take the form of a transportation commission reporting to the Speaker of the House. The premier and cabinet would decide how much money would be spent on transportation and where, in consultation with the commission, and the premier would have to explain to the House any deviation from the commission's recommendations. The commission could also monitor the execution of the program, as well as the performances of Crown corporations engaged in transportation activities, and keep an eye on the private companies now emerging with a government mandate in that field.

It is intriguing to speculate what might have happened if such control had existed in the early days of the province. First of all, Premier Turner would certainly not have started building his railway up the Bear River valley heading for an impassable glacier. Premier McBride might well have built all his railways in the right place, and

Premier Bennett would certainly not have started building a rail line to Dease Lake, nor would he have three-laned the Pat Bay Highway. Closer to our own time, Premier Bill Bennett would certainly not have imposed his nearly impossible and very expensive time limit on the construction of Phase 1 of the Coquihalla Highway, and the misconceptions about the cost overruns for that highway would not have occurred had the commission taken the time to correct the erroneous media reports. Most important of all, the fast-ferry fiasco might not have taken place. This solution, although ethical, might well not satisfy the egos and politics of B.C. premiers at times, but it would contain them, at least initially.

The above proposal is of course just one possibility; the people of British Columbia are open to suggestions. In the meantime, what they rather desperately ask of their premiers, now and in the future, is that there be less politics and more expertise in how their governments manage transportation and that there be at least some planning beyond the next election.

# Chapter Eight

## Final Report: 1999 to 2004

*"The party will eventually come to its senses and take a more moderate, transparent, fair and accountable course. I don't think (Premier) Gordon Campbell will be there."*
—Comments by MLA Paul Nettleton, B.C. Liberal member for
Prince George–Omineca, who was ousted from caucus
in 2002 for publicly condemning the Liberals'
moves towards privatizing B.C. Hydro

*"… a savage downsizing of the public service … "*
—George Heyman, BCGEU president, September 2003

As we have seen, B.C. politicians' tendencies to exploit their mandates by governing in favour of purely political preferences and objectives have been part of political life in the province from its beginnings. But have these patterns of action grown or decreased over the course of the years?

Neither Arthur Daniel Miller nor Ujjal Dosanjh, interim NDP premiers from August 1999 to February 2000 and February 2000 to June 2001 respectively, did much in the way of exploiting their mandate, although by inaction during their terms of office, both showed their approval of the fast-ferries project that went ahead under their watch. In addition to his brief term as premier after Clark's resignation in 1999, Dan Miller had been the minister responsible for ferries after Clark became premier in 1996. For his part, Dosanjh blocked requests for an inquiry into the fast ferries after he became premier in 2000. However, when the inevitable election came in June 2001, the NDP were disastrously reduced to two seats, the B.C. Liberals took power, and it soon became clear that under new premier Gordon Campbell, the practice of exploiting the mandate was remarkably alive and well.

As well as selling B.C. Rail and taking privatization to an extent never achieved to date, including the insidious, secretive, and piecemeal privatization of both B.C. Hydro and B.C. Ferries, the Campbell government proposed a refinement to this process that was quite unprecedented in British Columbia. In a trial balloon flown in 2003, Premier Campbell made it known that the government was considering leasing the Hope-to-Merritt section of the Coquihalla Highway to a successful applicant for a period of no less than 55 years. The company fortunate enough to win this prize would obtain the right to retain the tolls, in return, presumably, for the operation and maintenance of the roadway. What other benefits or requirements involved in this rather stupefying deal would accrue to or be laid against either side was not made clear.

What did become clear very soon was, firstly, the shock felt everywhere in British Columbia over the length of time of this proposed commitment by the government, and secondly, the rage and distress felt by all Interior residents, once they thought about the effect this could well have on their areas, particularly Merritt,

Kamloops, and Kelowna, the most directly affected. Whether the decision makers in Victoria thought about it or not, the people of B.C.'s Interior know full well the effects terrain and weather can have on a mountain highway, and particularly one passing over the Cascade Mountains.

Snowstorms, massive accumulations of snow, avalanches, ice storms, tumultuous rain, river flooding, mountain debris torrents, landslides, rock falls, rock and earth instability: they are all there, and they all, at some time or another, contribute to the gamble of opening a facility subject to them to public use, no matter what precautions are taken. Leasing, to the extent of relinquishing full control, which the government proposed in this case, also involves taking liability. A private company would be foolish not to insure itself adequately for these hazards. A moment's thought, at least by those people who knew about the hazards, brought the conclusion that the cost of the insurance could well raise the tolls if nothing else, as well as bring long closures, at times barely necessary. The voters of the Interior so impressed their Liberal office-holders with their absolute dissatisfaction with this proposal that the government quickly dropped it.

Much later in the year it became clear to those in the road-maintenance industry, especially those who had been ready to bid for the Coquihalla, that the government felt sorry about their losing a chance for such a lifetime reward and would make up for it. They were informed that all contracts for road maintenance to be renewed in 2004 would be of a 10-year duration, in place of the lesser lengths of time previously in force. No public announcements were made, since the government had learned about the dangers of these. (This of course would have been one more case of the province being bound to one political party's preferences by a legal contract of much longer duration than the subsequent governing group might enjoy.) Fifty-five years had been simply ridiculous; even10 years gave rise to concern. To those informed of the industry and of unpredictable factors such as oil prices, inflation, interest rates, etc., five years is a much preferable term for a road maintenance contract. Premier Campbell's strategy is obvious: He wants to make it very difficult and complicated for succeeding governments to change things. For example, if you cancel a 55-year contract when 5 years into it, do you have to compensate for 50 years' anticipated profits? The same question applies to 10-year road maintenance contracts, although for lesser numbers.

To strike a lighter note, one could argue that the government's change of heart came about because this premier had to make up for suddenly announcing early in the year that all roadside mowing was a thing of the past—an order that was apparently of his own initiation and one that had to be reversed in some regions later in the year due to the resulting fire hazard. [2]

The drive to satisfy what has become known as the "corporate culture" has not been limited to refinements in the privatization of Crown corporations and large public services, such as road maintenance. Proving that history always repeats itself, this drive has spread to the innermost civil service, reducing it in a manner even worse than that of the Great Depression. In the trend started by Bill Bennett and followed by Bill Vander Zalm, it is no less than the ultimate privatization of the public service, to an extent never previously envisioned.

In September 2003 the newspaper readers of Victoria were treated to the story of a civil servant who was described as "the deputy minister who oversaw the dramatic one-third reduction of B.C.'s public service."[3] It was said that he had brought about the disappearance of 12,000 government jobs, mostly in the last two years. This included what was described as a reshaping of the public service, otherwise labelled "a renewal culture" by a pilot of change named M.V. (Vince) Collins.

Vince Collins capped what was initially to be a 25-year career in the provincial civil service when he was appointed deputy minister of transportation and highways in 1988, a position he occupied for eight years. He was brought into highways by Premier Vander Zalm to implement the privatization of the highway maintenance function and other branches of the highways department, and there is no doubt that he did a competent job of what must have been a distasteful operation to any manager of human resources. He retired in 1996.

Collins was later rehired by the Campbell administration in the year 2001 as a member of the Liberal transition team. He said he came back primarily to do something about the "systemic malaise" that he saw in the public service, evidently arising subsequent to his departure. His mission, presumably, was to bring into being what he called a renewal culture to revitalize the dedication of the civil servants to serve the public better in the new era of privatization that had come to pass.

Some of the views in opposition to this, as put forward by BCGEU president George Heyman, were quoted in the aforementioned newspaper article: "The top ranks of the civil service may have bought in to the renewal culture, but for most public servants morale is at an all-time low as they look to more cuts in the push to privatization. I know he wanted to revitalize the public service, but the reality is that the job he was brought in to do was a savage downsizing of the public service. When most of our members hear about a public service renewal they laugh. It is a cruel joke."

Vince Collins' comment about all of this (in the same article), after he said that it was hard not to be compassionate for anyone who loses their job, was, "You can only bring about change when you get people to buy in." He also described how he had eased the departure of unwanted civil servants, including those of long service, by buying them out by way of a generous early-retirement program.

The one vital fact seemingly overlooked by those who advocate this drastic downsizing and privatizing of the provincial civil service in this "renewal culture," is that experience and expertise in managing British Columbia also went out the door with that tempting early retirement package—knowledge of B.C.'s unique challenges, gained from long service on the job and passed on by those who went before. To quote Donald J. Savoie, author of *Breaking the Bargain: Public Servants, Ministers, and Parliament,* good civil servants have "expertise and memory and require anonymity and permanence to do their job." There is little doubt that public service privatization, when taken to excess, removes or at least seriously depletes many of these resources.

There is also little doubt that there is a problem within this provincial government, which Collins and the governing politicians seem to feel requires this public-service renewal. However, the problem could stem from other reasons, as another correspondent to the Victoria press noted in a letter to the editor in September 2003.[4] The writer, a retired civil servant named Mike Stewart, was deploring the constant putdown of the civil service by a local radio broadcaster who was using the carefully selected statistics so readily provided by the Fraser Institute, which Stewart describes in his letter as "nothing more than an entirely bought-and-paid-for propaganda vehicle for big corporations."[5]

His conclusion was that British Columbians should think carefully about whether or not they want this campaign against the civil service to continue—and behind this may be the thought, held by many, that the "systemic malaise" mentioned by Collins is due to the service losing its most able and experienced people, and as this continues, more and more criticism of it will arise. It is a vicious downward spiral. The letter writer's final words were, "The constant denigration of government and government services by a self-serving corporate culture is the problem. Maybe we should start looking at that issue to see how divisive and damaging it has been to our society as a whole—in this province and elsewhere."

These arguments raise the following question: Are the terms "renewal culture" and "corporate culture" one and the same? Only time will tell. In any event, it seems that Collins is leaving his job of dismantling and revitalizing the civil service before the task has been completed. In other words, the pilot is leaving the B.C. ship of state in mid-voyage. Let us all hope that it comes in to a happy landing.

The key to it all is the captain of the ship, the premier, and whether or not he can pursue a steady course for the benefit of all—in other words, govern fairly, reward work not wealth, and act for the many, not the few. At the time of this writing it is apparent to those not obsessed with the corporate culture that Premier Campbell is engaged in a progressive dismantling of the B.C. civil service and a wholesale disposal of the province's Crown corporations. When the irreversibility of these moves is considered, there is no doubt that we are now seeing the greatest mandate exploitation of them all. Campbell's reign carries the taste of incipient anarchy, something that Bob Williams speculated about in 1972; Campbell may well achieve it. He should remember the example of Bill Bennett, which is that B.C. will put up with a dog that barks, but not with one that howls.

He soon shocked the province with the severity of his first legislative moves, particularly Bill 29, the Health and Social Services

Delivery Act. Two legal and properly processed agreements with two of the largest unions in the province, reached with the aid of an industrial inquiry commissioner and a mediator, were peremptorily thrown out by a succeeding government—this by an Act containing a clause stating that no action for damages or compensation may be brought against the government or any person because of it. The Liberals obviously considered these agreements to be sweetheart deals between the unions and the NDP, and they may well have been right. The union members were offered a compromise agreement and voted against it.

However, should the NDP come to power in the future and try the same thing with the privatization agreements signed by this Liberal government and the private companies involved, one can only surmise that a similar exculpatory clause would promptly be taken to the courts, and compensation would very likely be awarded in full measure. As long as moves and countermoves like this continue, there will always be turmoil at the top in the provincial government. It would be better for British Columbia for a provincial government to strike a balance between these two extremes. There are many voters in B.C. these days, liberals with a small "l," who wish that this would happen.

The discontent between people and governments evident everywhere these days is well summed up in a musing by the internationally respected Canadian philosopher John Ralston Saul, who also happens to be the consort of the Governor General of Canada. He has said that "the authentic life of the individual has been gravely distorted by 'corporatism,' the domination of public life by corporate bodies of business and professional, academic and political groups, both left and right, whose special interests override the citizen's interest in the public good." There has only been one premier in recent British Columbia history who, for the most part, has stood aside from this: his name, of course, is W.A.C. Bennett.

In a speech in New York in July of 1929, Franklin Delano Roosevelt, then the governor of the state of New York, addressed the problem of liberty. He called for supplementing the ancient doctrine of separation of church and state with an absolute separation of government and business.[6] Including unions along with business in the separation would make this a perfect formula for British Columbia. To further paraphrase Roosevelt, then there could be a social government, not a socialistic one.

But political change in British Columbia depends on many things—that more of its population interest themselves in politics and exercise their franchise, especially younger people of voting age; that there be democracy within political parties, as well as better candidates chosen in a fairer way; and that the plotting of the province's course will be made by those whom the people elect, not those the premier appoints.

Certainly in many cases, our premiers' motivations for exploiting their mandates in favour of their political preferences may have been the advancement of society and the enhancement of the lives of British Columbians. However, the recent revelation that the Liberal Party in British Columbia has received $14.8 million over the past four years from the business community and that the New Democratic Party has received $1.1 million from the unions,[7] brings to mind the thoughts recently made by Justice Sandra Day O'Connor of the American Supreme Court:

> Just as troubling to a functioning democracy as classic quid pro quo corruption is the danger that officeholders will decide issues not on their merits or the desires of their constituencies, but according to the wishes of those who have made large financial contributions valued by the officeholder. And, unlike straight cash-for-votes transactions, such corruption is neither easily detected nor practical to criminalize. The best means of prevention is to identify and remove the temptation.[8]

Amen, Justice O'Connor—and bravo, Jean Chrétien, for ending your career as a lawmaker with legislation to restrict campaign contributions. In Canada, only Quebec and Manitoba have abolished corporate and union contributions to political parties. As surely as the sun rises and sets, Canadians, and more specifically British Columbians, will sooner or later shake themselves, find a middle path, make a few compromises, and end up all right. Let it be sooner rather than later.

# Appendix A

## A Report to Alec Fraser

Early in 1985, Minister of Transportation and Highways Alec Fraser received a report before the highway construction was finished. Fraser was provided with the attached map and other maps, photographs, and ancillary information to illustrate the avalanche threat.

The report also provided reasons for exceeding the original estimate of $250 million for Phase 1. The minister decided to stay with the original published estimate at that time, although it is notable that the report contains a revised estimate of $400 million for Phases 1 and 2.

The Boston Bar Creek valley was the last section to be completed in 1986. The sites of some of the proposed avalanche containment basins first had to be cleared of the overburden of soil and decayed vegetation, which in many places was much deeper than expected. Underlying this in some places were closely packed boulders of two and three metres size and more, which proved to be very difficult to excavate, especially with the time constraint. Because of this, some sites for avalanche containment basins were abandoned and some avalanche diversion trenches were bermed instead of excavated.

This and other difficulties encountered led to a dearth of borrow. Hundreds of thousands of cubic metres of blasted rock had to be hauled from two quarries, one each side of Box Canyon, in order to attain the raised grade for the highway essential to clear the winter pack of snow. This contributed substantially to the overruns on many of the Boston Bar Creek valley contracts, as well as claims from other contractors for through-haul interference, as there was no road up the Boston Bar Creek valley, only the tote roads put in by each contractor. Nonetheless, the final grade was built to full height and width, and many of the special features were installed.

The point to be taken from all of this is that, had he taken a full explanation to the public, Alec Fraser had ample and legitimate reasons for amending the estimate. He did not do this because he did not wish to embarrass his premier. He could not foresee that a subsequent premier, of his own party, would subject his actions to a commission of inquiry.

The following is a verbatim copy of the short version of the report to Minister Fraser. Before he left office the minister gave his permission for this to be so used.

### The Coquihalla Story: 1985

A favourite thought of the earliest road builders in British Columbia, the Royal Engineers, was without doubt the old adage "the shortest way between two points is a straight line" as it is to the modern day airline navigators as they plot their great circle courses over the North Pole.

The Engineers were frustrated however when they tried to find a direct straight line route to the bottom south-west corner of the Province from the interior by the tendency of the mountains to trend north or north-west from the U.S. border. The river valleys tended that way too, and the frustration increased when they realised how difficult it was to build by way of the greatest river of them all— through the Fraser River Canyon.

There was one notable exception however, a route using the valleys of the Coquihalla River and the Coldwater River, which aligned themselves almost due north-east pointing directly at the hub of the interior transportation routes, then and now, the Kamloops area.

But when Lieutenant Lempriere R.E. explored this route in the early winter of 1849 he sensed right away the "Achilles heel" of this most favourable alignment—probably from the very early snow cover at the higher altitudes—and he reported: "I do not consider it desirable that this trail … be formed into a carriageway."

A few years later a Royal Engineer's sergeant whilst surveying and mapping the area noted "the signs of fearsome snow falls in the defiles of the Coquihalla" and thus confirmed the first known reluctance to challenge these "fearsome snow falls" of the Coquihalla Pass.

Nevertheless, twenty-five years later, the first settlers of the Douglas Lake cattle country, which is close to the present day town of Merritt again cast eyes upon this direct way to the head of navigation on the lower Fraser River. They prevailed upon the Commissioner of Lands and Works at that time, the Honorable Forbes George Vernon, Member of Assembly, and cattleman, from the interior city now named after him, to build a six foot wide cattle trail from Nicola Forks (Merritt) to Hope by the valleys of the Coldwater and Coquihalla Rivers.

Although quite unsung in history this was clearly the first of the series of remarkable feats of construction carried out on this route. In light of the means available to them then it is hard to believe today how they built this trail with pick axes and wheelbarrows through the long and high slides of "huge fragments of broken rock" that Vernon reported.

Just as remarkable is the fact that they maintained the trail in good order for almost forty years after its construction in 1876. It was not used in winter of course, and only sporadically in summer when they drove bands of cattle through, westbound to market and eastbound to improve the breeding stock. The trail existed until it was destroyed by the construction of the Kettle Valley Railway, opened in 1916, through the very same pass.

The fever of railway building which seized Canada in the early 1880s and which lasted till the mid-1920s did not ignore the Coldwater-Coquihalla way through the Cascade Mountains. The irony is that the railway builders did not build the rail line initially from Merritt to Hope, they used the Coquihalla Pass to get from Princeton, much further south of Merritt, as part of a route from the southern boundary area of British Columbia to the lower mainland. They did not use the route for its directness—they used it because they found they could get a grade of not more than 2.5% by the Coquihalla valley.

To get such a grade they found, later, that they had to undertake construction in the lower Coquihalla valley which was so difficult that it required what was literally inspired railway engineering to overcome. They also found out even before they had opened the rail line to passenger traffic that the problems of maintenance, especially in winter, were far from insignificant.

This realization came to them in the winter of 1915-16 the very winter before they were scheduled to open the line to passenger traffic at the end of July 1916. That winter experienced the unbelievable snowfall of 67 feet, the greatest ever registered before or since. The line was closed by massive snow slides from mid-November to late March, and miles of timber snowsheds that had been constructed the year before were rendered into matchwood.

It was not, however the snowfall that finally defeated the railwaymen (although it helped). The closure of the last of the rich copper mines in the Similkameen watershed combined with the opening of the Hope-Princeton Highway in 1949 did that. The railway outlasted that latter detriment for a little over ten years but finally carried its last train on November 23, 1959.

Two years before that the construction of a natural gas pipeline commenced, and it was subsequently "looped" into two pipelines. This installation pioneered the use of the Boston Bar Creek valley as an alternative to the upper Coquihalla valley as a transportation route.

Then the Trans-Mountain Oil Pipe Line came into existence and this pipeline used the upper Coquihalla valley as its route after the railway was dead, taking over parts of the railway grade, either for the pipeline itself or for the access road. By the mid-sixties both these pipeline companies were using the overall route and combining in the use of a single access road where they were together in the same stretch of valley.

One vital thing must be remembered—even though the gas pipeline experienced the severe snowfalls of the Boston Bar valley, which were never as severe as in the past, there is a big difference between maintaining a buried pipeline which can be inspected by helicopter, and maintaining a highway. Additional burying by the avalanche runouts can be tolerated provided there is no damage to the pipeline. Their problems came when there was damage to the pipelines!

Finally in 1973 the Department of Highways, becoming concerned by the traffic increase in the Fraser Canyon section of the Trans-Canada Highway, started a reconnaissance survey through the Coquihalla Pass with the intention of designing a highway. They chose the same route as the gas pipeline and went through the Boston Bar Creek valley, despite its 67 avalanche paths.

This reconnaissance was followed by a complete survey which commenced in 1978 and was complete to Kingsvale from Hope by 1982.

This survey completion was not a reality before the first construction contract was called in 1979, but construction lingered. Only three out of 25 contracts were completed or under way before the Cabinet decided to rush the completion of this 120 kilometre highway to completion in less than two years—a section of highway which normally would have taken at least ten years to build.

This decision was taken in the spring of 1984, and the completion deadline was the opening of Expo 86 in May of 1986. It appears that this deadline (at least to the month mentioned) will be met. Paving will need to the end of May 1986 to complete.

The challenge of the speedy construction has been met—it now remains to see if the challenge of the tremendous snowfalls, as experienced in the past, will be met. Presuming of course that these snowfalls return with the ferocity that they had in the first half of this century.

To ensure that this challenge is in fact overcome the Ministry of Transportation and Highways has instituted what is undoubtedly a quite remarkable program of avalanche protection for the avalanche prone area, which is almost exclusively that portion of the highway through the Boston Bar Creek valley.

When this programme is considered it must be borne in mind that many things have changed since the railwaymen fought the same conditions in 1915. They themselves experienced change during their period of maintenance. Costs and difficulties were so bad in the Thirties, even with cheap labour, that it was only the wartime traffic that prevented a total close down—the 1930s saw year after year of above average snowfalls. After the war the advent of the gasoline

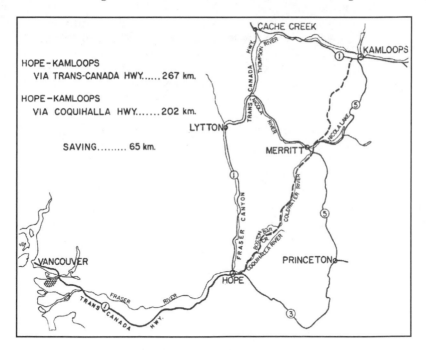

## The Coquihalla Highway Map

The above map was contained in the report given to Alec Fraser in 1985. It shows the highway in its original conception as an alternative to the Trans-Canada highway between Hope and Kamloops, to be built in two phases, separated by Merritt. It does not show Phase 3 of the final system. That phase, eventually called The Okanagan Connector, was a later addition. This explains why Fraser only issued estimates initially for Phase 1 and Phase 2, from Hope to Kamloops, and he never did issue an estimate for Phase 3. This of course was a major cause of the confusion that arose later when his estimates for Phase 1 and Phase 2 were compared to the final cost of all three phases.

powered tracked bulldozer gave a new lease of life to the harassed snow removal crews. Finally of course the railway closed anyway.

From 1945 to 1949 when the Hope-Princeton Highway was being built the equipment that was used was very different from that which the contractors have available to them now. Then a mobile power shovel, or excavator, or loader that had a bucket of one cubic yard capacity was considered huge—now such shovels or loaders have buckets up to six cubic yards in capacity—a six cubic yard shovel makes a man beside it look like a Lilliputian. In 1949, and even in 1959 an eight foot diameter steel pipe culvert was considered very large. Today under the Coquihalla Highway they are installing elliptical steel pipes of 37 feet in width as vehicle underpasses. Besides these men look very small indeed.

The point of all this is to emphasize that in the construction of the Coquihalla Highway the road building industry of British Columbia has really come of age. Where twenty years ago repeated excavations of 25,000 cubic yards would have been onerous, nowadays repeated excavations of 250,000 cubic yards are readily undertaken. The total excavation of all materials for the Coquihalla Highway will be about 40 million plus cubic yards—for the Hope-Princeton Highway, slightly longer but albeit two lanes only, the total excavation was five million cubic yards. The Hope-Princeton took twice as long to build.

The further extension of this is that in 1959 when the railway breathed its last, the concept of building an avalanche diversion trench in the ground at the foot of it, 180 metres wide and 200 metres long and 5 to 10 metres deep, and beside it a rock fill berm 150 metres long and 30 metres high would have been considered the ideas of a crazy man. Similarly the building of a series of avalanche containment basins all two or three acres in area and totalling a quarter of a million cubic yards of excavation in large boulders would have been thought foolhardy in the extreme. Now such are being done and by them it is considered that an active avalanche path more than a thousand metres long and 200 metres wide can be controlled—the thundering snow can be diverted—and a condition that in 1959 would have been one where men were helpless to control can now be controlled.

Where such control is not possible and by necessity the highway must climb high into the very track of such an avalanche, the traveller will be held safe by a structure to contain the roadway and roof it over for one thousand feet, such roof of such incredible strength as to withstand the blows of snow debris and boulders falling on it to depths of forty feet from heights of three thousand feet.

Better still than to simply withstand the full fury of the sliding snow are the measures realized in recent years to forecast avalanches

These are the signs of "fearsome snowfalls" (avalanche paths or tracks) that Lieutenant Arthur Lempriere of the Royal Engineers saw in 1859 when he blazed a trail up the Boston Bar Creek valley while trying to find an acceptable way from Fort Hope to Boston Bar without going through the lower Fraser Canyon. The constant movement of snow prevents the growth of trees and the paths show white with the snow. The lieutenant wisely looked elsewhere for a route, and the wagon road was built from Yale to Boston Bar alongside the Fraser River. The cause of this excess of snowfall is the movement of moisture-laden clouds in storms flowing in from the Pacific Ocean up the lower valley of the Fraser, then following the Coquihalla and Boston Bar Creek valleys until they come up against the high mountain ridge (Zopkius Ridge) at the head of the latter. The view is of the western slope of the Boston Bar Creek valley.

and to trigger them before the build up of snow in their starting zones is such as to let them reach their full ferocity.

This then is the story of the Coquihalla Highway. That the saving of the directness of its route between Hope and Kamloops is realizable despite the difficulties of the extreme snow falls.

This is the gamble that has been made by the construction of the highway for a total bill of over $400 million.

The answer to the wager lies in the future—the engineers of today are confident to the extreme that they have the Coquihalla beaten. Talking about Lilliputians however gives a funny feeling when the profile of the Great Bear Avalanche path is studied in its entirety—the Great Bear Snowshed looks Lilliputian!

# Appendix B

## Premiers and Times of Service

1. John Foster McCreight
   November 1871 to December 1872
2. Amor De Cosmos
   December 1872 to February 1874
3. George Anthony Walkem
   February 1874 to January 1876
4. Andrew Charles Elliot
   February 1876 to June 1878
5. George Anthony Walkem
   June 1878 to June 1882
6. Robert Beaven
   June 1882 to January 1883
7. William Smithe
   January 1883 to March 1887
8. Alexander Edward Batson Davie
   April 1887 to August 1889
9. John Robson
   August 1889 to June 1892
10. Theodore Davie
    July 1892 to March 1895
11. John Herbert Turner
    March 1895 to August 1898
12. Charles Augustus Semlin
    August 1898 to February 1900
13. Joseph Martin
    February 1900 to June 1900
14. James Dunsmuir
    June 1900 to November1902
15. Edward Gawler Prior
    November 1902 to June 1903

16. Richard McBride
    June 1903 to December 1915
17. William John Bowser
    December 1915 to November 1916
18. Harlan Carey Brewster
    November 1916 to March 1918
19. John Oliver
    March 1918 to August 1927
20. John Duncan MacLean
    August 1927 to August 1928
21. Simon Fraser Tolmie
    August 1928 to November 1933
22. Thomas Dufferin Pattullo
    November 1933 to December 1941
23. John Hart
    December 1941 to December 1947
24. Byron Ingemar Johnson
    December 1947 to August 1952
25. William Andrew Cecil Bennett
    August 1952 to August 1972
26. David Barrett
    September 1972 to December 1975
27. William Richards Bennett
    December 1975 to August 1986
28. William Vander Zalm
    August 1986 to April 1991
29. Rita Margaret Johnston
    April 1991 to November 1991
30. Michael Franklin Harcourt
    November 1991 to February 1996
31. Glen David Clark
    February 1996 to August 1999
32. Arthur Daniel Miller
    August 1999 to February 2000
33. Ujjal Dosanjh
    February 2000 to June 2001
34. Gordon Muir Campbell
    June 2001

## Chief Commissioners of Lands and Works

Col. R.C. Moody, 1858; C. Brew, 1863; J.W. Trutch, 1864; B.W. Pearce, 1871; H. Holbrook, 1871; G.A. Walkem, 1872; R. Beaven, 1872; F.G. Vernon, 1876; G.A. Walkem, 1878; R. Beaven, 1882; W. Smithe, 1883; F.G. Vernon, 1887; G.B. Martin, 1895; C.A. Semlin, 1898; F.L. Carter-Cotton, 1899; J.S. Yates, 1900; W.C. Wells, 1900; R. McBride, 1903; R.F. Green, 1903; R.G. Tatlow, 1906; F.J. Fulton, 1907

## Ministers of Public Works

T.Taylor,1908; C.E.Tisdall,1914; J.H.King,1916; H.W.Sutherland, 1922; N.S. Lougheed, 1928; R.W. Bruhn, 1929; R.H. Pooley, 1932; W. Savage, 1933; F.M. MacPherson, 1933; T.D. Pattullo, 1939; C.S. Leary, 1939; T. King, 1941; R.W. Bruhn, 1941; J. Hart, 1941; H. Anscomb, 1942; E.C. Carson, 1946; E.T. Kenney, 1952; P.A. Gaglardi, 1952

## Ministers of Highways

P.A. Gaglardi, 1955; W.A.C. Bennett, 1967 (also Premier); W.D. Black, 1968; R.M. Strachan, 1972; G.R. Lea, 1973; A.V. Fraser, 1975

## Minister of Highways and Public Works

A.V. Fraser, 1977

## Minister of Transportation, Communications and Highways

A.V. Fraser, 1978

## Ministers of Transportation and Highways

A.V. Fraser, 1980; C. Michael, 1986; C.S. Rogers, 1987; N. Vant, 1988; R.M. Johnston, 1989; L. Hanson, 1991; A. Charbonneau, 1991; J. Pement, 1993; C. Evans, 1996; L. Boone, 1996; H. Lali, 1998; H. Giesbrecht, 2001

## Ministers of Transportation

J. Reid, 2001; K. Falcon, 2004

*Dates indicate first year in office*

# Chapter Notes

## Preface

1. Black, "British Columbia: the Politics of Exploitation," From *British Columbia: Patterns in Economic, Political and Cultural Development*, Dickson Falconer (ed.), pp, 251, 261.
2. Sherman, *Bennett*, p. viii.

## Chapter One

1. Ormsby, *British Columbia: A History*, p. 252.
2. Titley, *The Frontier World of Edgar Dewdney*, pp. 22-31.
3. Jackman, "Hon. Amor de Cosmos," From *British Columbia: Patterns in Economic, Political and Cultural Development*, Dickson Falconer (ed.), p. 220.
4. Titley, *The Frontier*, p. 31.
5. Harvey, *The Coast Connection*, p. 60.
6. Harvey, *The Coast*, pp. 59, 66.
7. Harvey, *Carving the Western Path By River, Rail, and Road Through B.C.'s Southern Mountains*, p. 53.
8. Ibid.
9. Ibid. pp. 51-54.
10. Ormsby, *British Columbia*, pp. 309-11.
11. Roy, "Progress, Prosperity and Politics: the Railway Policies of Richard McBride." From *British Columbia: Patterns in Economic, Political and Cultural Development*, Dickson Falconer (ed.), p. 224.
12. Norcross, *Nanaimo Retrospective*, p. 58.
13. Rayner, *Premiers in Profile*, pp. 68, 71.
14. Sanford, *McCulloch's Wonder: The Story of the Kettle Valley Railway*, pp. 33-35.
15. Ibid. p.35.
16. Harvey, *Carving the Western Path By River, Rail, and Road Through B.C.'s Southern Mountains*, p. 69; Sanford, *McCulloch's Wonder*, pp. 35-36.
17. Harvey, *Carving … Southern Mountains*, pp. 68-69, pp. 143-50; Sanford, *McCulloch's Wonder*, pp. 35-36.
18. Sanford, *McCulloch's Wonder*, pp. 38-45.
19. Turner, *Sternwheelers and Steam Tugs: An Illustrated History of the*

      *Canadian Pacific Railway's British Columbia Lake and River Service*, pp. 69-98.

20.  Ormsby, *British Columbia*, pp. 318-20.

21.  Harvey, *Carving … Central and Northern B.C.*, pp. 15-25.

22.  Ibid. p. 144.

23.  Ormsby, *British Columbia*, p. 304.

24.  Ibid. p. 383.

25.  Ibid. pp.319-24; Rayner, *Scandal!!*, pp. 33-43.

26.  French, *The Road Runs West*, pp. 31-36, 218, 245; Rayner, *Scandal!!* pp. 220-24.

## Chapter Two

1.  Harvey, *Carving the Western Path By River, Rail, and Road Through Central and Northern B.C.*, pp. 49-73.

2.  Roy, "Progress, Prosperity and Politics: the Railway Policies of Richard McBride." From *British Columbia: Patterns in Economic, Political and Cultural Development*, Dickson Falconer (ed.), p. 226.

3.  Ormsby, *British Columbia: A History*, pp. 345-48.

4.  Ibid.

5.  Roy, "Progress," pp. 226-33.

6.  Harvey, *Carving … Central and Northern B.C.*, pp. 66-67.

7.  Roy, "Progress," pp. 228-31.

8.  Ibid.

9.  Sanford, *McCulloch's Wonder: The Story of the Kettle Valley Railway*, pp. 148-60.

10.  Harvey, *Carving the Western Path By River, Rail, and Road Through B.C.'s Southern Mountains*, pp. 107-30.

11.  Roy, "Progress," pp. 238-44.

12.  Ibid.

13.  Ormsby, *British Columbia*, p. 406.

14.  Roy, "Progress," p. 242; Ormsby, *British Columbia*, p. 365.

15.  Harvey, *The Coast Connection*, pp. 73-74.

16.  Harvey, *The Coast*, pp. 87-88.

17.  Ormsby, *British Columbia*, p. 430.

18.  Harvey, *The Coast*, p. 86.

19.  Harvey, *Carving … Southern Mountains*, pp. 178-80.

20.  Ormsby, *British Columbia*, p. 325.

## Chapter Three

1.  Ormsby, *British Columbia: A History*, p. 439.

2.  Ibid. p. 433.

3.  Minister of Public Works Annual Report 1929-1930, pp. T6, T112-115; Harvey, *The Coast Connection*, p. 107.

4. MacDonald, *A Critical Growth Cycle for Vancouver, 1900-1914*. From *British Columbia: Patterns in Economic, Political and Cultural Development*, Dickson Falconer (ed.), p. 55.

5. Minister of Public Works Annual Report, 1933-34, p. 3.

6. Woodcock, *British Columbia: A History of the Province*, p. 217.

7. Minister of Public Works Annual Report, 1936-37, pp. X3, X4.

8. *Vancouver News Herald*, June 20, 1938, "Sitdowners stage riot: 23 jailed, 100 men hurt."

9. Ibid.

10. Harvey, *The Coast Connection*, pp. 111-13.

11. Ormsby, *British Columbia*, p. 461.

12. Minister of Public Works Annual Report, 1938-39, pp. Z57-Z128.

13. Ormsby, *British Columbia*, pp.470-71, 475; Mitchell, *W.A.C. Bennett*, pp. 62-64. The Rowell Sirois Commission recommended widespread centralization of power and that financial control be taken away from the provinces and placed in Ottawa. Pattullo opposed it strongly and suffered thereby.

14. Hodgson, *Squire of Kootenay West*, pp. 78, 85.

15. Harvey, *Carving the Western Path By River, Rail, and Road Through Central and Northern B.C.*, p. 101.

16. Ibid.; Ormsby, *British Columbia*, p. 465.

17. Harvey, *The Coast*, pp. 121-25.

18. Anscomb, Herbert, unpublished diary.

19. Worley, *The Wonderful World of W.A.C. Bennett*, pp. 185-86.

## Chapter Four

1. Sherman, *Bennett*, pp. vii-viii., 242-43, 250, 259-60, 272-77; Worley, *The Wonderful World of W.A.C.Bennett*, p. 243.

2. Worley, *The Wonderful World*, p. 139.

3. Mitchell, *W.A.C. Bennett*, pp. 260-67; Sherman, *Bennett*, pp. 175-76.

4. Mitchell, *W.A.C. Bennett*, p. 182.

5. Ibid. p. 363; Sherman, *Bennett*, pp. 176-78.

6. Mitchell, *W.A.C. Bennett*, pp. 373-75.

7. Shelford, *From Snowshoes to Politics*, pp. 165-66.

8. Harvey, *The Coast Connection*, p. 144.

9. B.C. Ministry of Highways Annual Report, 1958/59, p. G38; Sherman, *Bennett*, p. 185.

10. Mitchell, *W.A.C. Bennett*, pp. 404, 414.

11. B.C. Ministry of Highways Annual Reports, year 62/63 pp. 29,102; 63/64 pp. 29,107; 65/66 pp. 25, 109; 66/67 pp. 29, 109; 67/68 pp. 26, 111. Projects, 1288, Lot 5181-Usk; 1291, Copper River Approaches; 1360, Copper River to Usk; 1459, Terrace to Copper River; 1616, Boulder River to Hell's Bells Creek; 1617, Hell's Bells Creek to Lot 5181.

12. Worley, *The Wonderful World*, p. 146; Mitchell, *W.A.C. Bennett*, pp. 208-09.

13. Harvey, *The Coast*, p. 200-201; Harvey, *Carving the Western Path By River, Rail, and Road Through Central and Northern B.C.*, p. 20.
14. Mitchell, *W.A.C. Bennett*, pp. 278-81.
15. Ibid. pp. 415-30.
16. Kavic and Nixon, *1,200 Days–A Shattered Dream: Dave Barrett and the NDP in B.C. 1972-75*, p. 48.
17. Ibid. pp. 54-55; Morley *et al*, *The Reins of Power*, p. 154.
18. Shelford, *From Snowshoes*, p. 166 *passim*.
19. Kavic and Nixon, *1,200 Days*, p. 45, note 13.
20. Ibid. p. 47.
21. Ibid. p. 54.
22. Ibid. pp. 220-21.

## Chapter Five

1. Garr, *Tough Guy: Bill Bennett and the Taking of British Columbia*, p. 21; Persky, *Son of Socred*, pp. 44-48.
2. Nichols and Krieger, *Bill Bennett: The End*, pp. *16, 17*.
3. Harvey, *The Coast Connection*, pp. 187-94.
4. Mitchell, *Succession: The Political Reshaping of British Columbia*, pp. 32-33, 41-42; Allen White, "Bennett Fires Jack Davis," *The Province*, April 4, 1978.
5. Mitchell, *Succession*, p. 39.
6. Garr, *Tough*, pp. 31-34, 42-46; Mitchell, *Succession*, pp. 39, 47-49, 52.
7. Garr, *Tough*, pp. 82-83; Mitchell, *Succession*, pp. 56-57.
8. Blake *et al*, *Grassroots Politicians*, pp. 7-8; Garr, *Tough*, pp. 90-94, 111-12.
9. Black, "British Columbia: The Politics of Exploitation," From *British Columbia: Patterns in Economic, Political and Cultural Development*, Dickson Falconer (ed.), pp. 249-55.
10. Garr, *Tough Guy*, pp. 103-106.
11. Ibid. pp.116-22; Mitchell, *Succession*, pp. 62-63.
12. Garr, *Tough Guy*, pp. 122-23, 131-32; Mitchell, *Succession*, pp. 65-66.

## Chapter Six

1. Mitchell, *Succession: The Political Reshaping of British Columbia*, pp. 125-27.
2. Persky, *Fantasy Government*, pp. 39-40.
3. Blake *et al*, *Grassroots Politicians*, pp. 99-111; Mitchell, *Succession*, pp. 92-124.
4. Persky, *Fantasy*, pp. 28-29; Keith Baldrey, *Vancouver Sun*, June 16, 1986.
5. Persky, *Fantasy*, pp.30-31; Mitchell, *Succession*, pp. 40-41, 106-107.
6. Persky, *Fantasy*, pp. 22-23, 63; Mitchell, *Succession*, p. 43.
7. Harvey, *The Coast Connection*, p. 201.

8. Reksten, *The Illustrated History of British Columbia*, p. 260.
9. Mackay, *Report of the Commissioner Inquiry into the Coquihalla and Related Highway Projects*, pp. 14-16.
10. Alec Fraser turned this report over to the author at the time he left the office of minister and gave verbal permission at that time for the author to use it as he pleased.
11. B.C. Ministry of Transportation and Highways Annual Reports, fiscal years 1986-87 and 1987-88.
12. Valerie Casselton and Keith Baldrey, *Vancouver Sun*, August 28, 1987, p. B2 and Sept. 17, 1987.
13. Gary Mason, *Vancouver Sun*, Nov. 3, 1987, p. 1; Trevor Lautens, *Vancouver Sun*, Nov. 14, 1987, p. B9.
14. *Times Colonist*, April 3, 1991, p.1; Les Leyne, *Vancouver Sun*, March 12, 1991; Les Leyne and Richard Watts, *Vancouver Sun*, April 5, 1991, p. D13.
15. Burton, *et al. A Preliminary Report on the Operational, Human Resource and Financial Implications of the Privatized Highway Maintenance Program of the Province of British Columbia*, p. 54. "In summary, the Review Team's research into the cost of the Ministry's original program and the cost of the privatized program has yielded the conclusion that the privatized program has cost more than would have been the case had the Ministry's original program continued unchanged."

## Chapter Seven

1. *Times Colonist*, October 13, 1995, pp. A1, A6.
2. Rayner, *Scandal!!*, pp. 196-207; *Times Colonist*, Nov. 16, 1995.
3. Harvey, *The Coast Connection*, pp. 144-45.
4. Memo to file dated May 30, 1973, entitled "Report on Nanaimo-Vancouver Ferry Route Relocation" (no file number) signed by the assistant deputy minister, acknowledged by the deputy minister.
5. B.C. Ministry of Transportation and Highways, *A Transportation Planning Overview for the Province of British Columbia*, Volume 14, Ferry System, pp. 14-16.
6. Rayner, *Scandal!!*, pp. 13-22.
7. "Fixed link not realistic, report finds," *Times Colonist*, December 17, 2002.
8. "$20-million sale final chapter in fast ferry fiasco," *Times Colonist*, March 25, 2003, pp. A1, A2.
9. Rayner, *Scandal!!*, pp. 21-22.

## Chapter Eight

1. Jeff Rud, "Paul Nettleton: Legislature Outcast," *Times Colonist*, December 7, 2003, page D1.
2. Premier Campbell's other mistake in the matter of transportation was

much more personal and precedent setting. While on holiday in Hawaii early in January 2003, he was charged with driving under the influence of alcohol. He pled guilty, was fined, and ordered to get counselling. His blood-alcohol reading was later reported as high. The premier apologized to the people of British Columbia for this occurrence in a television broadcast.

3. Judith Lavoie, "B.C.'s Pilot in a Storm," *Times Colonist*, September 7, 2003, p. D5.

4. *Times Colonist*, letter to the editor from Mike Stewart, Comox, B.C., September 8, 2003, p. A7.

5. *Times Colonist*, September 23, 2003, p. A6. In September of 2003, the Fraser Institute issued a press release based on a report from the Ontario director of policy studies asserting that lower levels of young driver fatalities in Ontario and Alberta would be reversed if public insurance took over. Both reports failed to include the fact that both Ontario and Alberta had introduced legislation restricting the number of young drivers on the road in the period of time studied.

6 Black, *Franklin Delano Roosevelt*, p.194. Any student of present-day B.C. politics would be wise to read Conrad Black's masterpiece, more specifically the part dealing with the 1930s. Here he tells of Roosevelt's utter contempt for businessmen acting as politicians and how they very nearly put the economy of the western world right under. The worst of them, including Hoover, never conceded that Roosevelt's enlightened policies saved the United States from utter disaster. Roosevelt was himself a very poor businessman, but he was an outstanding leader and a superb politician. Adam Smith's comment of 1776, "that the government of an exclusive company of merchants is perhaps the worst of all governments" is just as true today as when he said it. The exception is of course W.A.C. Bennett, but he did not surround himself with businessmen as Hoover did.

7. Adrian Dix, "Special interests threaten democracy," *Times Colonist*, January 5, 2004, p. A6. Dix is a former adviser to the NDP government.

8. Ibid. Dix is quoting the comments of Justice O'Connor issued with the finding of the U.S. Supreme Court upholding the McCain-Feingold Campaign Finance Reform Law, which limits special-interest spending in the elections.

# Bibliography

Bakan, Joel. *The Corporation: The Pathological Pursuit of Profit and Power.* Toronto: Viking Canada, 2004.

B.C. Minister of Highways Annual Reports. 1955/56–1975/76.

B.C. Ministry of Highways and Public Works Annual Reports. 1976/77–1977/78.

B.C. Ministry of Public Works Annual Reports.1924/25–1954/55.

B.C. Ministry of Transportation and Highways Annual Reports. 1980/81–1985/86.

B.C. Ministry of Transportation, Communications and Highways Annual Reports. 1978/79–1979/80.

B.C. Ministry of Transportation and Highways. *A Transportation Planning Overview for the Province of British Columbia,* Volume 14, Ferry System. Victoria, B.C.: Delcan, 1988.

Black, Conrad. *Franklin Delano Roosevelt.* New York: Public Affairs, Perseus Book Group, 2003.

Black, Edwin R. "British Columbia: The Politics of Exploitation." From Dickson M. Falconer (ed.), *British Columbia: Patterns in Economic, Political and Cultural Development.* Victoria, B.C.: Camosun College, 1982.

Blake, Donald E., R. Kenneth Carty, and Lynda Erickson. *Grassroots Politicians.* Vancouver: UBC Press, 1991.

Burton, Peter, Ron Parks, Kevin McCulloch (Ernst & Young), and Robert G. Harvey. *A Preliminary Report on the Operational, Human Resource and Financial Implications of the Privatized Highway Maintenance Program of the Province of British Columbia.* Victoria, B.C.: Government of B.C., 1994.

Falconer, Dickson M. (ed.). *British Columbia: Patterns in Economic, Political and Cultural Development.* Victoria, B.C.: Camosun College, 1982.

French, Diana. *The Road Runs West: A Century Along the Bella Bella/Chilcotin Road.* Madeira Park, B.C.: Harbour Publishing, 1994.

Garr, Allen. *Tough Guy: Bill Bennett and the Taking of British Columbia.* Toronto: Key Porter Books, 1985.

Harvey, R.G. *The Coast Connection.* Lantzville, B.C.: Oolichan Books, 1994.

——.*Carving the Western Path by River, Rail, and Road Through B.C.'s Southern Mountains.* Surrey, B.C.: Heritage House, 1998.

——.*Carving the Western Path by River, Rail, and Road Through Central and Northern B.C.* Surrey, B.C.: Heritage House, 1999.

Hodgson, Maurice. *The Squire of Kootenay West*. Saanichton, B.C.: Hancock House, 1976.

Jackman, Sydney W. "Hon. Amor de Cosmos." From Dickson M. Falconer (ed.), *British Columbia: Patterns in Economic, Political and Cultural Development*. Victoria, B.C.: Camosun College, 1982.

Kavic, Lorne J. and Brian Nixon. *The 1,200 Days–A Shattered Dream: Dave Barrett and the NDP in B.C. 1972-75*. Coquitlam, B.C.: Kaen Publishers, 1978.

MacDonald, Norbert. *A Critical Growth Cycle for Vancouver, 1900-1914*. From Dickson M. Falconer (ed.), *British Columbia: Patterns in Economic, Political and Cultural Development*. Victoria, B.C.: Camosun College, 1982.

MacKay, Douglas L. *Report of the Commissioner Inquiry into the Coquihalla and Related Highway Projects*. Victoria, B.C.: Crown Publications, 1987.

Mason, Gary and Keith Baldrey. *Fantasyland: Inside the Reign of Bill Vander Zalm*. Toronto: McGraw-Hill Ryerson, 1989.

Mitchell, David J. *W.A.C.Bennett and the Rise of British Columbia*. Vancouver: Douglas & McIntyre, 1983.

———. *Succession: The Political Reshaping of British Columbia*. Vancouver: Douglas & McIntyre, 1987.

Morley, J. Terence, Norman. J. Ruff, Neil A. Swainson, R. Jeremy Wilson, and Walter D. Young. *The Reins of Power: Governing British Columbia*. Vancouver: Douglas & McIntyre, 1983.

Nichols, Marjorie and Bob Kreiger. *Bill Bennett: The End*. Vancouver: Douglas & McIntyre, 1986.

Norcross, E. Blanche (ed.). *Nanaimo Retrospective. The First Century*. Nanaimo, B.C.: Nanaimo Historical Society, 1979.

Ormsby, Margaret A. *British Columbia: A History*. Toronto: MacMillans, 1958.

Persky, Stan. *Fantasy Government: The Fall of Bill Vander Zalm and the Future of Social Credit*. Vancouver: New Star Books, 1989.

———. *Son of Socred*. Vancouver: New Star Books, 1979.

Rayner, William. *Scandal!! 130 Years of Damnable Deeds in Canada's Lotus Land*. Surrey, B.C.: Heritage House, 2001.

———. *British Columbia's Premiers in Profile: The Good, the Bad and the Transient*. Surrey, B.C.: Heritage House, 2000.

Reksten, Terry. *The Illustrated History of British Columbia*. Vancouver: Douglas & McIntyre, 2001.

Roy, Patricia E. "Progress, Prosperity and Politics: The Railway Policies of Richard McBride." From Dickson M. Falconer (ed.), *British Columbia: Patterns in Economic, Political and Cultural Development*. Victoria, B.C.: Camosun College, 1982.

Sanford, Barrie. *McCulloch's Wonder: The Story of the Kettle Valley Railway*. West Vancouver, B.C.: Whitecap Books, 1979.

Savoie, Donald J. *Breaking the Bargain: Public Servants, Ministers, and Parliament*. Toronto: University of Toronto Press, 2003.

Shelford, Cyril. *From Snowshoes to Politics*. Victoria, B.C.: Orca Books, 1987.

Sherman, Paddy. *Bennett*. Toronto: McClelland and Stewart, 1966.

Titley, Brian. *The Frontier World of Edgar Dewdney*. Vancouver: UBC Press, 1999.

Turner, Robert D. *Sternwheelers and Steam Tugs: An Illustrated History of the Canadian Pacific Railway's British Columbia Lake and River Service*. Victoria, B.C.: Sono Nis Press, 1984.

Woodcock, George. *British Columbia: A History of the Province*. Vancouver: Douglas & McIntyre, 1990.

Worley, R.B. *The Wonderful World of W.A.C. Bennett*. Toronto: McClelland and Stewart, 1971.

## Newspapers

*The Province* (Vancouver)

*The Vancouver Sun*

*Times Colonist* (Victoria)

*Vancouver News Herald*

# Index

# Photo Credits

Heritage House Collection: 13, 14, 16, 17, 20, 22, 23, 26, 27, 28, 31, 35, 36, 40, 49, 50, 51, 52, 55, 60, 64, 77, 80, 81, 86, 99, 100, 101, 106, 125, 138, 139, 141, 142
B.C. Ministry of Transportation and Highways: 41, 53, 61, 65, 70-71, 87, 107, 127, 145, 147
R.G. Harvey: 8, 79, 144, 148-49, 173, 175, 192
Darlene Nickull: 151
Ted Hughes: 135

Photographs included in this book have been donated or purchased from various sources and are reprinted based on conditions of use at the time of purchase.

# The Author

Bob Harvey joined the British Columbia Department of Public Works in 1948. A provincially licensed professional engineer since 1950, he graduated with a degree in civil engineering from the University of Glasgow, Scotland, in 1943. He served in the British armed forces from 1943 to 1947 and is a member of the Military Engineers' Association of Canada. From 1948 to 1954 he was an engineer on road construction and then a district engineer in the east and west Kootenays. Finally he advanced to regional maintenance engineer in the southwest corner of the province. In 1958 he became regional highway engineer at Prince George, where he was responsible for all provincial highways north of Williams Lake.

In 1967 he was moved to Victoria and put in charge of maintenance and building of terminals for the newly created B.C. Ferries Corporation. He advanced to senior bridge engineer, senior design engineer, assistant deputy minister, and finally deputy minister of highways in 1976. He retired in 1981.

His career gave him an inside view of highways ministers Phil Gaglardi and Alec Fraser and premiers W.A.C. Bennett and W.R. Bennett. He has written three books on the history of transportation in British Columbia.